JOHN BURKE

IMAGINE
THE
GOD
OF
HEAVEN

FIVE SESSIONS ON
NEAR-DEATH EXPERIENCES,
GOD'S REVELATION, AND THE LOVE
YOU'VE ALWAYS WANTED

TYNDALE
elevate
ask. seek. find.

Visit Tyndale online at tyndale.com.

Tyndale and Tyndale's quill logo are registered trademarks of Tyndale House Ministries. *Tyndale Elevate* and the Tyndale Elevate logo are trademarks of Tyndale House Ministries. Tyndale Elevate is a nonfiction imprint of Tyndale House Publishers, Carol Stream, Illinois.

Imagine the God of Heaven Study Guide: Five Sessions on Near-Death Experiences, God's Revelation, and the Love You've Always Wanted

Cover designed by Dean H. Renninger

Edited by Christine M. Anderson

Published in association with Don Gates of the literary agency The Gates Group; www.the-gates-group.com.

For information about special discounts for bulk purchases, please contact Tyndale House Publishers at csresponse@tyndale.com, or call 1-855-277-9400.

ISBN 978-1-4964-7994-5

Printed in the United States of America

29	28	27	26	25	24	23
7	6	5	4	3	2	1

Contents

From John Burke

WELCOME TO THE STUDY GUIDE AND VIDEO SERIES for *Imagine the God of Heaven*!

This study guide is designed to help you dive deeper into God's Word based on what you read in the book and watch on the videos. It is a study about God—his marvelous, loving attributes—and how you relate to the one who created you for himself. In the videos, you will meet some people from the book who had near-death experiences (NDEs) and hear what they discovered about the character and attributes of the God of the Bible.

Maybe you have questions or concerns about near-death experiences and/or the Bible. You may be skeptical about whether near-death experiences should even be considered valid testimonies of God's identity. Or perhaps you're fascinated by near-death experiences but don't really trust the Bible. Whatever the case, I invite you to approach this study with an open mind. If you do, I believe many of your questions will be answered. I've also included an FAQs section in the back of this study to address some of these questions directly.

Our study together will give you a comprehensive understanding of God's great love story told in the Bible, his awe-inspiring attributes, and how God wants to relate to you personally. I hope the videos, which feature firsthand testimonies of people who have experienced NDEs, will bring the God of Scripture to life for you in new ways. As you will see, even those who clinically died, were resuscitated, and came back to tell of God's unending beauty and inconceivably great affection for us struggle to find adequate words to describe their experience.

This study looks through the lens of Scripture to interpret NDEs. The admonition of Scripture is to "set your sights on the realities of heaven, where Christ sits in the place of honor at God's right hand. Think about the things of heaven, not the things of earth" (Colossians 3:1-2). NDE testimonies help us do just that—to see and imagine the reality of the God of heaven and all that Christ has promised for those who love him, so that we live for God. These stories don't supplant the Bible, but they can function as commentaries to it, helping us better imagine what God has revealed in Scripture. They can boost our faith just as testimonies from other faithful believers do. And, as it is with any testimony about an experience of God, it's wise to evaluate what we hear based on God's revelation in Scripture.

This study guide and accompanying video series are designed for a five-week Bible study experience. Although it is conceived for use by groups, it is quite useful for individual study as well. Each session begins with a group study that includes Scripture, video teaching and stories, and group discussion. Group sessions are designed for a 75-minute meeting but can be easily adapted for a 60- or 90-minute meeting. See the Facilitator's Guide (page 120) for additional guidance in adapting times. To help you apply what you're learning about God between group meetings, sessions also include five personal studies for individuals. Each of these can be completed in about fifteen minutes.

Throughout the next five weeks, I hope you will be enthralled by hearing the testimonies of those who describe the wonders of the God of heaven revealed in Scripture and that the fire of your faith will burn brighter than ever. That's my prayer for you—that you would know and love God with all your heart as you realize that he loves you more than you can imagine.

God's blessings,
John Burke

Study Guide Overview

WELCOME

You are about to begin an exciting journey through the *Imagine the God of Heaven* small group Bible study. During the next five weeks, we will enjoy an in-depth exploration of God's wonders and how we relate to God. Nothing is more important than the way we imagine God because the way we view God affects every decision we make about how we live today.

THE BOOK AND VIDEO

This study guide and video curriculum are based on the book, *Imagine the God of Heaven: Near-Death Experiences, God's Revelation, and the Love You've Always Wanted*. After the first session, you'll see that the theme of each session aligns with one of the four parts of the book. Although we will not cover all the material in the book chapter by chapter, we will explore the four themes in a practical and deeper way.

Each of the five group sessions includes a fifteen-minute video featuring comments from John Burke and testimonies from some of the people you'll read about in the book.

GROUP STUDY FORMAT

The *Imagine the God of Heaven* video series and study guide are designed to be experienced in a group setting (such as a small group gathering or

Sunday school class) but can also be adapted for individual study. Each group session begins with questions for reflection and Scripture passages. The remainder of the session includes video teaching, a directed discussion on the video teaching and testimonies, and a closing prayer. Feel free to adapt the format to the size and structure of your group or for individual use.

Everyone in the group should have their own copy of this study guide as well as the *Imagine the God of Heaven* book. Why? Because it helps all members to actively engage in group discussions, to complete the five personal studies, and to benefit from the content in the book. Also, keep in mind that the video and discussion questions are simply tools to help you engage with the session. The real transformation comes from digging into Scripture and engaging with the God of Scripture as you're learning.

In meetings, group members are encouraged to share how they are learning and engaging with God during the week. This might include talking about failures or struggles as well as wins and new learnings, because both are necessary for any authentic relationship to grow. Groups should have a facilitator to help create a safe environment in which questions, doubts, concerns, struggles, and victories are all welcome. The facilitator is responsible for leading the meeting, starting the video, and keeping track of time during discussions. Facilitators may also prompt participants to contribute to ensure that everyone has the opportunity to participate. For additional guidance, see the Facilitator's Guide (page 119).

INDIVIDUAL STUDY

Every group session is followed by five personal studies designed to lead you into a deeper engagement with the theme of that session. Each personal study includes Scripture reading, reflection questions, and a suggested focus for prayer to deepen your communication with God. If your group meets every other week rather than weekly, you can adapt the personal studies simply by spacing them out to every other day.

IMAGINE THE GOD OF HEAVEN

OPEN

A pastor named A. W. Tozer once wrote, "What comes into our minds when we think about God is the most important thing about us."[1] One of the amazing things about God is that he wants to be known. He has revealed himself throughout the Bible, in the life of Jesus, and in all kinds of other ways. In this study, we will consider how God's revelation in Scripture aligns with what we learn about God from those who have had near-death experiences (NDEs). Whether you're just exploring faith in God or have followed God for years, the goal of our time together will be to know God more so we can love him more.

Questions

1. Which of the following images comes closest to describing how you imagined God when you were a child?

   - Policeman God. *God is an eye in the sky, always trying to catch you doing something wrong.*

   - Grandpa God. *God is retired from doing his work, kind of senile, and basically out of commission.*

   - Hidden God. *God is uninvolved, distant, and unknowable.*

   - Marine Sergeant God. *God is a stern, impossible-to-please taskmaster.*

   - Mr. Rogers God. *God is a slipper-wearing sweetheart, always ready with a smile and an encouraging word.*

   - Loving Parent God. *God is a tender, kind, sometimes correcting, always caring parent in heaven.*

2. Now that you are older, what image comes to mind when you think about God? How is it similar to or different from your childhood image of God?

3. If what A. W. Tozer wrote is true—that what we think about God is the most important thing about us—what implications might that have for you? In other words, how might the way you imagine God now impact how you see yourself? Treat other people? Understand the world at large?

READ

The Word [Jesus] gave life to everything that was created,
   and his life brought light to everyone.
The light shines in the darkness,
   and the darkness can never extinguish it.

God sent a man, John the Baptist, to tell about the light so that everyone might believe because of his testimony. John himself was not the light; he was simply a witness to tell about the light. The one who is the true light, who gives light to everyone, was coming into the world.

JOHN 1:4-9

This is the message we heard from Jesus and now declare to you: God is light, and there is no darkness in him at all. So we are lying if we say we have fellowship with God but go on living in spiritual darkness; we are not practicing the truth. But if we are living in the light, as God is in the light, then we have fellowship with each other, and the blood of Jesus, his Son, cleanses us from all sin.

1 JOHN 1:5-7

Questions

1. According to the passage from 1 John, if we have a relationship with God, we will no longer live in spiritual darkness but instead will live in the light.

   - *Based on your own experience, how would you describe what it means to live in spiritual darkness?*

   - *Based on your own experience, how would you describe what it means to live in spiritual light? For example, how did you first encounter the light of God, and what changed in your life as a result?*

2. Why do you think Jesus is called "the true light"?

3. Why is it important that Jesus came into the world to give light "to everyone"?

WATCH

Watch the Session 1 video and take notes on your reflections and questions.

"How could I explain so many people, clinically dead, with no heartbeat, no brain waves, yet when resuscitated, they come back saying similar things?"

"Paul said, 'I was caught up to the third heaven' (2 Corinthians 12:2)."

*"Why do you think we are hearing more of these
near-death experiences today?"*

DISCUSS

1. What thoughts, feelings, or questions did watching the video bring up for you?

2. John Burke admits that he initially struggled to believe in NDEs. What, if anything, makes it difficult for you to believe in NDEs?

3. NDE testimonies do not equate with God's revelation of himself in Scripture. However, they do add color to the picture God has already given of himself in the Bible. In what ways, if any, do NDE testimonies enhance your image of God?

4. When Christians talk about God, they often mention that God is all loving, all knowing, and all powerful, but not that he is light. Yet, it is the light of God that NDErs so often comment on. What do you think this means, and why does it matter that God is light?

5. If NDEs are God's gift to the world, how might these experiences fit with the idea that Jesus came to bring the light of God into the world so everyone can know him?

CLOSE
Encouragement

We have a God of light in whom there is no darkness. God wants to cleanse us from our sin, give us fellowship with one another, and ultimately make his eternal home with us. That is a God worth knowing and who is impossible not to love!

Prayer

> Invite God to give you a passion to seek him,
> to know him, and to share him with others.

 This coming week: Read chapters 1–3 of *Imagine the God of Heaven* and complete the personal studies.

FROM SKEPTICAL TO CONVINCED

In *Imagine the God of Heaven*, John Burke writes that he was initially skeptical about near-death experiences (NDEs) but became convinced through his research, in which he discovered that millions of people have reported having NDEs and that their stories have incredible commonalities. Not only that, but many doctors have become convinced because of patients who described what they experienced while clinically dead, including details that would otherwise have been impossible for them to know.

READ

One of the twelve disciples, Thomas (nicknamed the Twin), was not with the others when Jesus came. They told him, "We have seen the Lord!"

But he replied, "I won't believe it unless I see the nail wounds in his hands, put my fingers into them, and place my hand into the wound in his side."

Eight days later the disciples were together again, and this time Thomas was with them. The doors were locked; but suddenly, as before, Jesus was standing among them. "Peace be with you," he said. Then he said to Thomas, "Put your finger here, and look at my hands. Put your hand into the wound in my side. Don't be faithless any longer. Believe!"

"My Lord and my God!" Thomas exclaimed.

Then Jesus told him, "You believe because you have seen me. Blessed are those who believe without seeing me."

JOHN 20:24-29

REFLECT

1. How would you describe your view of NDEs? Are you skeptical, convinced, or uncertain? If skeptical or uncertain, what questions do you have? If convinced, what was it that convinced you?

2. John Burke writes, "Over the past thirty-five years, I've interviewed countless individuals and studied thousands of NDE reports. . . . I've since become convinced that NDEs are God's gift to our world—evidence of God's great love for all people" (*Imagine the God of Heaven*, page 24). If it's true that NDEs are a gift from God to reveal his love, in what ways have the NDE stories you've read and watched helped you to experience or understand some new insight about God's love?

3. In the passage from the Gospel of John, Thomas, who had on multiple occasions heard Jesus predict his death and resurrection, refused to believe the other disciples' testimonies that Jesus had in fact risen from the dead. When Jesus later appeared to Thomas, Jesus could have reprimanded Thomas for his doubts, but he didn't. Instead, he gave Thomas exactly what he needed to believe.

- What role, if any, has doubt played in your own spiritual journey?

- How has Jesus shown himself to you and given you what you needed to move from doubt to faith? Or how do you wish he would reveal himself to you to help you with your doubts?

If, like Thomas, you still have doubts about Jesus, know that he welcomes your questions and invites you to seek the truth about who he is. Though he does not make it a practice to just "show himself" as we often think he should, he does respond to our desire to seek him and know him better in ways that are personal to each of us.

- Start by praying, "God, if you're real, let me know it. Show yourself to me."
- Consider the evidence for Jesus and his resurrection. There are many great books that address questions about the Christian faith in a systematic way, often referred to as apologetics. Or you can search online for answers by googling "apologetics websites" or checking out GotQuestions.org. Later in Imagine the God of Heaven, you'll read some of the evidence for Jesus, specifically the Old Testament prophecies he fulfilled.
- Ask a knowledgeable Christian friend or pastor to meet with you so you can ask questions.

4. God has always built people's faith through the stories or testimonies of others. And those stories have power. In fact, in recounting his vision of a great heavenly battle in which Satan was defeated, the apostle John heard a loud voice in heaven declare, "And they have defeated him by the blood of the Lamb *and by their testimony*" (Revelation 12:11, emphasis added). Some of the most powerful testimonies in the Bible, such as those from Isaiah, Ezekiel, Paul, and John, offer us a glimpse of heaven.*

- *How would you describe the power or impact of NDE testimonies, especially those that describe heaven?*

- *How have NDE testimonies encouraged your faith or challenged your lack of faith?*

RESPOND

Take a moment to reflect on the ways God has revealed himself to you, recently or in the past. What are you especially grateful for? Thank him for demonstrating his love for you in these ways and invite him to continue building your faith or meeting you in your doubts in the weeks ahead.

---

* See Isaiah 65:17-25; Ezekiel 43:1-12; 2 Corinthians 5:1-10; 12:1-4; Revelation 21:1-5.

DAY 2

FOUND BY YOU

"Many NDErs come back and seek to learn more about the God of Light, but others do not. God gives us the choice to seek him or ignore him. It's also important to note that just because an NDEr sees God does not mean that person knows God or is necessarily right with God." *Imagine the God of Heaven*, page 15

READ

"If you look for me wholeheartedly, you will find me. I will be found by you," says the LORD.
JEREMIAH 29:13-14

Keep on asking, and you will receive what you ask for. Keep on seeking, and you will find. Keep on knocking, and the door will be opened to you. For everyone who asks, receives. Everyone who seeks, finds. And to everyone who knocks, the door will be opened.
MATTHEW 7:7-8

REFLECT

1. Why do you think some people (NDErs or not) seek God and others don't?

2. God promises, "If you look for me wholeheartedly, you will find me." The two Hebrew words translated "wholeheartedly" are *kol* and *lebab*. *Kol* means "all, everything, totality." *Lebab* means "heart." In the Jewish understanding, *heart* can refer to the entire inner person, the "self, the seat of thought and emotion."[2] With this understanding in mind, how would you characterize your wholeheartedness—the degree to which you are seeking and following God in this season of your life? Circle the number on the continuum that best describes your response.

1   2   3   4   5   6   7   8   9   10

I am not at all   I am completely
wholehearted.   wholehearted.

* *Briefly describe why you responded as you did.*

* *What, if anything, is holding you back from a wholehearted pursuit of God? Why?*

3. Jesus confirmed the promise that God wants to be found by assuring us that, "Everyone who seeks, finds."

* *What does it tell you about God that he stays "hidden" to those who don't seek him, yet he makes himself knowable to those who truly want to know him?*

- *In Matthew 7:7, Jesus used the phrase "keep on" three times: "keep on asking," "keep on seeking," "keep on knocking." To keep on is to continue, to never stop. How might God be inviting you to keep on asking, seeking, and knocking for whatever it is you need most from him right now?*

4. What person has God put in your life who you think is open to seeking him? How could you be a help to them? What if you asked them to join you in reading *Imagine the God of Heaven*?

RESPOND

God promises, "If you look for me wholeheartedly, you will find me." In what personal struggle, relationship, or circumstance do you most need to find God and experience God right now? Share your heart with God and ask him to help you seek him wholeheartedly, holding nothing back.

ALL PEOPLE OF ALL NATIONS

"I am convinced God created all people in his image, and he is *for* all people of all nations. NDErs confirm God speaks to them in their native languages. This God sees all, knows all, wants to forgive all, and unconditionally loves each person uniquely. If you will keep an open mind and follow me on this journey of imagining God, I hope you'll see that a loving relationship, not religion, is actually what God wants with you and me." *Imagine the God of Heaven*, page 20

READ

The LORD had said to Abram, "Leave your native country, your relatives, and your father's family, and go to the land that I will show you. I will make you into a great nation. I will bless you and make you famous, and you will be a blessing to others. I will bless those who bless you and curse those who treat you with contempt. All the families on earth will be blessed through you."
GENESIS 12:1-3

Many nations will join themselves to the LORD on that day, and they, too, will be my people.
ZECHARIAH 2:11

After this I saw a vast crowd, too great to count, from every nation and tribe and people and language, standing in front of the throne and before the Lamb. They were clothed in white robes and held palm branches in their hands. And they were shouting with a great roar,

"Salvation comes from our God who sits on the throne
    and from the Lamb!"
REVELATION 7:9-10

REFLECT

1. God chose Abram (later called Abraham) not just to be blessed but to be a blessing—a blessing to "all the families on earth." What does that tell you about God?

2. Though the Old Testament is mostly about the Israelites (the descendants of Abraham), we repeatedly see God's heart for everyone, as affirmed in Zechariah 2:11 above. Why do you think it might have been important for God to remind the Israelites that he was for everyone, not just them?

3. Just as God chose Abraham for an important mission, God has also chosen you and given you a similar mission—to be a blessing to others by serving and loving them and by helping them to know God and his love. To fulfill his mission and receive God's promise, Abraham first had to leave behind everything that was certain and familiar to him, including the blessings he already had—his country, his relatives, his father's family.

   • *How would you describe the spiritual truth or principle behind what God required of Abraham, that he first had to leave everything behind?*

- *What implications might that same spiritual truth or principle have for you? In other words, what certain and familiar things might God ask you to leave behind or let go of so you can be a blessing to others?*

4. God's heart is for all people and all nations.

   - *What do you think are some signs that a person's heart is aligned with God's heart? For example, how might that be evident in the way a person prays, spends money, allocates their time, or chooses their friends?*

   - *How would you assess yourself in these same areas? In what ways is your heart most or least aligned with God's heart for all people and all nations?*

5. In Revelation 7, we see that heaven will be filled with people "from every nation and tribe."

   - *What about that makes you excited? What, if anything, makes you nervous or uncomfortable?*

- *If God's Kingdom sons and daughters will come from every tribe and nation, how might we align ourselves and prepare ourselves for that kind of eternity even now?*

Over the next few weeks, consider taking one of the following steps to grow your heart for people outside of your culture or nation:

- *Pick a country to pray for every day.*
- *Go out of your way to meet and get to know someone of a different race, culture, or nationality.*
- *Ask someone who has a very different ethnic and cultural background from you to go to lunch or come over for dinner.*
- *Look into opportunities to go on a cross-cultural serving trip.*
- *Read a biography of (or study online about) a cross-cultural Christ-follower such as Hudson Taylor, William Carey, Elisabeth Elliot, or Adoniram Judson.*

RESPOND

God's heart is that people from all nations will come to faith. Ask God to help you align your heart with his heart in every area of your life. Invite him to show you how you can be a blessing to others this week.

FOR A PURPOSE

"About the time human history began to be widely recorded, God claimed to do something to bless all people. Around 2000 BCE, God chose two people through whom he would create a 'chosen nation.' The word *chosen*, though, is sometimes misunderstood. *Chosen* does not mean 'loved more' or 'better than' but rather 'set apart for a purpose.' . . .

"When God created the 'chosen' Jewish nation, he did so to bless all people in two ways. First, he revealed his heart, his character, and his will through many Jewish prophets so that we can know and love him as he loves us. Second, he made the incredible and radical prophetic promise that he would send the Messiah, the Savior for all humanity, to bless all nations for all time. As you will see throughout this book, NDErs around the globe meet this same 'I Am' that Jesus claimed to reveal (John 8:58)." *Imagine the God of Heaven*, pages 46–47

READ

> He said to me, "You are my servant, Israel,
>> and you will bring me glory."
> I replied, "But my work seems so useless!
>> I have spent my strength for nothing and to no purpose." . . .
> And now the LORD speaks—
>> the one who formed me in my mother's womb to be his servant,
>> who commissioned me to bring Israel back to him. . . .
> He says, "You will do more than restore the people of Israel to me.
>> I will make you a light to the Gentiles,
>> and you will bring my salvation to the ends of the earth."
> ISAIAH 49:3-6

Starting with Abraham, the nation of Israel was chosen by God. They were chosen to be a light to all the nations, a conduit of God's message and love. But over time, they took being chosen as being better than other nations and saw themselves as the sole recipient and keeper of God's message and love. Isaiah expresses his dismay that Israel had failed to fulfill its purpose when he declares that his work is "useless," "for nothing and to no purpose." In response, God speaks of another Servant, who would accomplish what his servant Israel could not. This new Servant would not only restore the people of Israel but be "a light to the Gentiles" to bring salvation to the ends of the earth. This is a reference to the Messiah, whom Isaiah says will be killed to pay for our sins and bring salvation to all the nations (see Isaiah 52:13–53:12). Jesus is that Messiah, and when he came to earth, he declared God's love for *all* nations and scolded the Israelites for their ethnocentric, nationalistic, selfish chokehold on God and his blessings.

> When Jesus heard this [the faith of a Roman officer], he was amazed. Turning to those who were following him, he said, "I tell you the truth, I haven't seen faith like this in all Israel! And I tell you this, that many Gentiles will come from all over the world—from east and west—and sit down with Abraham, Isaac, and Jacob at the feast in the Kingdom of Heaven. But many Israelites—those for whom the Kingdom was prepared—will be thrown into outer darkness, where there will be weeping and gnashing of teeth."
> MATTHEW 8:10-12

> What sorrow awaits you teachers of religious law and you Pharisees. Hypocrites! For you shut the door of the Kingdom of Heaven in people's faces. You won't go in yourselves, and you don't let others enter either.
> MATTHEW 23:13

> "Yes," said Jesus, "what sorrow also awaits you experts in religious law! For you crush people with unbearable religious demands, and you never lift a finger to ease the burden."
> LUKE 11:46

REFLECT

1. Reread the passage from Isaiah and then put in your own words what God was saying to Israel.

2. What do you think might have led Israel to ignore God's words and instead view their "chosen" status as a sign that they were better than and should separate themselves from those who didn't know and follow God?

3. Just as the ancient Israelites misunderstood their status as God's chosen people, Christians today might also misunderstand what it means to be chosen by God.

   * *Many Israelites considered themselves to be better than non-Israelites and believed that God was only for them. In what ways do you recognize this same dynamic among Christians today?*

- Many Israelites chose to separate themselves from nonbelievers, ignoring God's command to share his love and mercy with them. In what ways have you seen Christians do the same?

- Instead of being for non-Israelites, the Israelites developed an "us vs. them" mentality. In what ways have you witnessed this same mentality among Christians today?

4. Now, let's make this personal.

- When have you found yourself thinking you are better than nonbelievers or that God isn't for them in the ways he is for you?

- In what ways, if any, have you separated yourself from nonbelievers?

- *When are you most likely to adopt an "us vs. them" mentality toward nonbelievers?*

5. What would have to shift in you for your heart to align with God's heart—to be truly *for* all people?

RESPOND

God wants you to have his heart for everyone so you will share his love, mercy, and kindness with everyone. Thank him for being patient with you and ask him to transform your heart so it becomes more and more like his.

INFINITE AND INTIMATE

Bibi Tahereh's story is featured in chapter 3 of *Imagine the God of Heaven*. A Muslim at the time, she suffered a heart attack and had an NDE in which she encountered a God who loved her and called himself "I Am." Bibi spent the next year seeking God and asking him to reveal himself to her. He did, and Bibi left Islam to follow Jesus.

READ

In Exodus 3, Moses is captivated by a burning bush and approaches it.

> When the Lord saw Moses coming to take a closer look, God
> called to him from the middle of the bush, "Moses! Moses!"
> "Here I am!" Moses replied.
> "Do not come any closer," the Lord warned. "Take off
> your sandals, for you are standing on holy ground. I am the
> God of your father—the God of Abraham, the God of Isaac,
> and the God of Jacob." When Moses heard this, he covered his
> face because he was afraid to look at God.
> EXODUS 3:4-6

When God gives Moses an assignment to go and speak for him, Moses asks who he should say sent him.

> God replied to Moses, "I Am Who I Am. Say this to the people
> of Israel: I Am has sent me to you." God also said to Moses,
> "Say this to the people of Israel: Yahweh, the God of your
> ancestors—the God of Abraham, the God of Isaac, and the
> God of Jacob—has sent me to you.

This is my eternal name,
   my name to remember for all generations."
EXODUS 3:14-15

The name "I Am" speaks to God's *infinite* existence—that he is uncreated and eternally existent. He reveals that he is "other than" or "holy." God is also *intimate*. He warned Moses not to come closer and to take off his sandals as this was holy ground. Yet, later, we see God repeatedly invited Moses to come closer and to experience intimacy with God, such as when the text says, "The LORD would speak to Moses face to face, as one speaks to a friend" (Exodus 33:11).

REFLECT

1. Briefly review the three passages from Exodus and write down what they reveal about who God is and how he engages Moses in relationship.

2. God is the great I Am. He is eternal, existing perpetually in the past, present, and future. In *Imagine the God of Heaven*, NDErs consistently say they met a God who is not bound by time. What implications might God being infinite have for the following?

   - *His love*

- *His forgiveness*

- *Your prayers*

- *His patience with you*

- *His timing in answering your prayers or acting in your life*

3. John Burke writes, "God is . . . *infinite*. He created time and space, so he exists outside the limits of our three-dimensional space. This means we can't physically go and 'find' God. For us to know God, he must intersect our time and space. In the Bible, God claims he has done this to bless and love all people" (*Imagine the God of Heaven*, page 47).

Because he exists outside time and space, God must choose to show up in our lives and, because he loves us, he does.

- *When did God first show up in your life? When and how did you recognize it was God engaging you?*

- *When has God recently intersected time and space to reveal himself to you, to speak to you by prompting your thoughts, or to help you to experience his presence? How did you recognize that it was God engaging you?*

4. God is infinite, and he is also intimate. God met with Moses face-to-face, as a friend. How would you characterize your experience of spending time with God? Do you feel like you're meeting face-to-face with a friend? Why or why not?

RESPOND

Take some time to be face-to-face with God. Praise him for being both infinite and intimate. Thank him for all the ways, large and small, that he has shown up in your life. Tell him how much it means to you that he wants to have an intimate relationship with you.

THE GOD OF ALL NATIONS

OPEN

If someone were to ask you, "Who is God for?" what would you say?

It's easy to answer that question with "God is for everyone." But what we tend to believe is more like "God is for me and people like me." Instead of an inclusive worldview that focuses on how God is for everyone, we default to an egocentric faith (how God is for us) and an ethnocentric faith (how God is for our own culture). We see this kind of faith in Jesus' original twelve disciples. They were often shocked and dismayed as they watched Jesus interact with those they rejected. For instance, Jesus said of a pagan Roman officer, "I tell you the truth, I haven't seen faith like this in all Israel! And I tell you this, that many Gentiles will come from all over the world—from east and west—and sit down with Abraham, Isaac, and Jacob at the feast in the Kingdom of Heaven" (Matthew 8:10-11). Jesus routinely interacted with Samaritans, tax collectors, immoral people, and Gentiles—all of whom were despised by the Jewish culture that shaped the disciples.

Questions

1. What might be some signs that a person's faith is egocentric or ethnocentric—that they believe God favors them or people like them over others?

2. Why do you think the twelve disciples struggled so much to truly believe God was for everyone and that Jesus wanted them to bring the gospel (the message of God's love and forgiveness) to people who were not like them?

3. Some would say that those who follow Jesus today still struggle to truly believe God is for everyone and wants all people to know him. What would you give as evidence that this is true or not true?

READ

The Lord had said to Abram, "Leave your native country, your relatives, and your father's family, and go to the land that I will show you. I will make you into a great nation. I will bless you and make you famous, and you will be a blessing to others. I will bless those who bless you and curse those who treat you with contempt. All the families on earth will be blessed through you."
GENESIS 12:1-3

Jesus came and told his disciples, "I have been given all authority in heaven and on earth. Therefore, go and make disciples of all the nations, baptizing them in the name of the Father and the Son and the Holy Spirit. Teach these new

disciples to obey all the commands I have given you. And be sure of this: I am with you always, even to the end of the age."
MATTHEW 28:18-20

The real children of Abraham, then, are those who put their faith in God.

What's more, the Scriptures looked forward to this time when God would make the Gentiles [the nations] right in his sight because of their faith. God proclaimed this good news to Abraham long ago when he said, "All nations will be blessed through you." So all who put their faith in Christ share the same blessing Abraham received because of his faith.
GALATIANS 3:7-9

Questions

1. Just as God told Abraham to be a blessing to all nations, Jesus told his followers to make disciples of all nations. How does the mission Jesus gave his followers continue the mission God gave Abraham? What connections do you see between these two statements?

2. How does Galatians 3:7-9 above help you to better understand God's promise to Abraham and his heart for all people?

3. How easy or difficult is it for you to show people of other cultures how God feels about them? Share the reasons for your response.

4. Briefly discuss what you learned from the chapters you read in *Imagine the God of Heaven*.

   • *What was your reaction to the stories about people from other countries and other religions who met Jesus in their NDEs? For example, did these stories surprise you? Confuse you? Excite you?*

   • *How does what you read align with or differ from your view of God up to this point?*

WATCH

Watch the Session 2 video and take notes on your reflections and questions.

*"When I was a skeptical engineer, one of the things
that opened my mind to near-death experiences
was the consistent descriptions of . . ."*

*"Jesus says, 'I am the light of the world. Whoever follows me will never
walk in darkness, but will have the light of life' (John 8:12, NIV)."*

*"How does your heart align with God's heart
for all people of all nations?"*

DISCUSS

1. What thoughts, feelings, or questions did watching the video
   bring up for you?

2. How does what you have read this week and watched on the video expand your view of God?

3. In what ways did watching the video strengthen your faith, lead you to love God more, or heighten your anticipation of heaven?

4. If you read a list of the top ten countries with the highest percentage of Christians, the United States is not one of them.[3] If you check out a list of the twenty countries where Christianity is growing the fastest, the United States is not one of them.[4] If you look up what country has the most missionaries sent to it, the United States is number one.[5] Although Christianity is global, the United States is not the center of it. In what ways does this information challenge you? In what ways does it encourage or excite you?

CLOSE
Encouragement

God told Abraham to be a blessing to all nations, and Jesus told his followers to make disciples of all nations—and it happened! People all over the world believe in and follow Jesus. But the mission is not done yet. So many still don't know him, and we are called to bring the good news to every corner of the earth and to all people!

Prayer

Pray this prayer from the Psalms aloud together:

> May God be gracious to us and bless us
> and make his face to shine upon us,
> that your way may be known on earth,
> your saving power among all nations.
> Let the peoples praise you, O God;
> let all the peoples praise you!
>
> PSALM 67:1-3, ESV

 This coming week: Read chapters 4–7 of *Imagine the God of Heaven* and complete the personal studies.

A TSUNAMI OF LOVE

The apostle John wrote, "God is love" (1 John 4:8). Love is not just a characteristic or disposition of God; love is who he is.

People who experience NDEs bring back the same message. Dr. Ron Smothermon says, "But [God's] light is more than light—it is overwhelming, a literal tsunami of infinite, unconditional love. All it touches transforms into perfect peace, and [it] blows away into irrelevancy any consideration about what is happening, replacing it with ineffable ecstasy, irresistible joy, love beyond comprehension—all in a singular package. A nuclear bomb blows life away. God's love blows death away" (*Imagine the God of Heaven*, page 61).

READ

I pray that from his glorious, unlimited resources he will empower you with inner strength through his Spirit. Then Christ will make his home in your hearts as you trust in him. Your roots will grow down into God's love and keep you strong. And may you have the power to understand, as all God's people should, how wide, how long, how high, and how deep his love is. May you experience the love of Christ, though it is too great to understand fully. Then you will be made complete with all the fullness of life and power that comes from God.

EPHESIANS 3:16-19

REFLECT

1. Write down what you learned about God's love from the Ephesians passage on the previous page. What impact does his love have on us?

2. Jesus said of all who love him, "My Father will love them, and we will come and make our home with each of them" (John 14:23). Here, in Paul's letter to the Ephesians, we see this idea again that "Christ will make his home in your hearts." Circle the statement below that best describes where you are currently in your spiritual journey.

   "Jesus is knocking, but I am not letting him in."

   "Jesus is an occasional visitor, but I usually don't let him stay too long."

   "Jesus has made his home in me and is a vital part of my life."

   "Jesus used to reside here, but not so much anymore."

   Other:

   Whatever your answer, what do you think Jesus is hoping will happen next when it comes to him making his home in you?

3. Paul prayed that "your roots will grow down into God's love and keep you strong."

   - *If someone who was new to faith asked you to explain how they could have their roots grow down into God's love, how would you respond? What might you suggest they do or not do?*

   - *How consistently are you doing those things that connect and establish you in God's love?*

4. We're told in Ephesians that God's love can "keep you strong" and make you "complete with all the fullness of life and power that comes from God."

   - *In what ways, if any, have you experienced God's love keeping you strong or making you complete? What is it like?*

- *In what circumstance or relationship would you like to experience more of God's love to keep you strong right now? What, if anything, might be holding you back?*

RESPOND

The God who knows you best loves you most. There is nothing you can do to make him love you more, and there is nothing you can do to make him love you less. He wants his unconditional, infinite love to come into your life like an overwhelming tsunami and make you full and complete. Express your gratitude to God for his empowering love, and ask him to help you sink your roots more deeply into his love in the week ahead.

LOVE COMES FROM GOD

God is love. God loves us. And God's love for us leads us to love others. In fact, Jesus said our love for others is the best evidence that our faith is real (Matthew 25:31-46) and the best way we can make our faith attractive (John 13:35).

John Burke writes, "God can lead us to love others with a God-sized kind of love, but only if we are willing. NDErs who have life reviews in God's presence consistently say, 'Little acts of loving-kindness matter to God'" (*Imagine the God of Heaven*, page 73).

READ

Dear friends, let us continue to love one another, for love comes from God. Anyone who loves is a child of God and knows God. But anyone who does not love does not know God, for God is love.

God showed how much he loved us by sending his one and only Son into the world so that we might have eternal life through him. This is real love—not that we loved God, but that he loved us and sent his Son as a sacrifice to take away our sins.

Dear friends, since God loved us that much, we surely ought to love each other. No one has ever seen God. But if we love each other, God lives in us, and his love is brought to full expression in us.

1 JOHN 4:7-12

We love each other because he loved us first.

If someone says, "I love God," but hates a fellow believer, that person is a liar; for if we don't love people we can see, how can we love God, whom we cannot see? And he has given us this command: Those who love God must also love their fellow believers.

1 JOHN 4:19-21

REFLECT

1. Why do you think it is so important to God that we love each other?

2. Sometimes Christians can struggle with . . .

   - Wanting to be right more than wanting to be loving. *In what ways do you recognize this struggle in yourself?*

   - Judging others instead of loving them. *Whom are you most likely to judge rather than love?*

- Being too focused on their own agenda to make time to actively demonstrate love to others. *In what ways or in what situations does busyness routinely undermine your ability to love?*

3. The apostle John states, "We love each other because he loved us first." Why do you think there is such a strong connection between being loved by God and being able to love others?

4. Mark an *X* on the continuums below to indicate your response to each of the statements.

I experience the love of God . . .

Never Rarely Occasionally Frequently Always

I am able to love others, even difficult people . . .

Never Rarely Occasionally Frequently Always

- *How do you understand the similarities or differences between your responses on the two continuums?*

- In Mere Christianity, author C. S. Lewis wrote that to love our neighbors as ourselves is not necessarily to feel fond of them but to wish their good—to want the best for them in the same way we want the best for ourselves.[6] What person or group of people do you find it most challenging to love right now? What makes it hard for you to want the best for them?

- Instead of trying hard to love others, perhaps the better strategy is to focus on experiencing God's love more. How might you meditate on the ways God loves you? How might you let God love you in this moment? In the day or week ahead?

RESPOND

It's amazing that God loves you *and* wants you to be a conduit of his love so others might experience it through you. Ask God to help you experience more of his love and to extend his love through you even to the hard-to-love people in your life. Pray the following prayer throughout the day and watch to see how God responds: "God, how do you want to love me today, and who do you want to love through me today?"

FREE TO CHOOSE LOVE

God is sovereign. That means he is "large and in charge." Yet our limitless God has chosen, in his sovereignty, some self-imposed limits. John Burke writes, "When God created everything out of nothing, every creative choice also came with self-imposed limits. God created humans to reflect his image, as in a mirror. Human beings could love, imagine, cocreate, and be united to God and each other, but this choice required one divine self-limitation—giving human beings free will. [Philip] Yancey writes, 'Of all God's creatures, [human beings] had a moral capacity to rebel against their creator. The sculptures could spit at the sculptor; the characters in the play could rewrite the lines.'[7] When God chose the medium of free will, he also chose the limitations that came with it. Why? Because of love. Love must be free to choose" (*Imagine the God of Heaven*, page 67–68).

READ

Today I have given you the choice between life and death, between blessings and curses. Now I call on heaven and earth to witness the choice you make. Oh, that you would choose life, so that you and your descendants might live! You can make this choice by loving the LORD your God, obeying him, and committing yourself firmly to him. This is the key to your life. And if you love and obey the LORD, you will live long in the land the LORD swore to give your ancestors Abraham, Isaac, and Jacob.

DEUTERONOMY 30:19-20

REFLECT

1. "Love must be free to choose."

   • *How would you explain why that is true? In other words, why is free will necessary for love?*

   • *If we didn't have free will, why would that prevent us from truly loving God?*

2. In the Deuteronomy passage, God offers his people the freedom to choose and encourages them to choose life. We choose life by loving, obeying, and committing ourselves to God.

   • *In what ways have you chosen life with your free will? Consider recent and past choices, small and large choices.*

   • *How would you describe the impact of the best life-giving choices you have made with your free will?*

3. In describing the consequences of giving human beings free will, Philip Yancey wrote, "The characters in the play could rewrite the lines."

IMAGINE THE GOD OF HEAVEN STUDY GUIDE

- In what ways have you have gone "off script" and used your free will in ways that weren't in line with God's loving plan? Consider recent and past choices, small and large choices.

- In what ways did these choices bring "death" instead of "life"? How would you describe the impact these choices had on you?

4. Using our free will to go against God and his will is called sin, and it makes us guilty before God. We deserve eternal separation from him, but because of his love for us, God provided a way for us to be reunited with him through Jesus' sacrifice on the cross. Jesus died in our place and was separated from God so we would no longer have to be.

   - How have you responded to God's offer?

   - How can you show your gratitude for what Jesus did for you? Thank him right now.

5. Using our free will to choose against the love of God is what poisons our lives and our world. Throughout human history, sinful choices are what has led to all the evil in the world, which sometimes leads us to wonder where God is and why he's not doing anything about it. But, as John Burke writes, "For a time, God stays partially hidden, allowing people to do very unloving

acts, but overcoming evil through willing people who freely choose to love and obey him. And despite all our evils and abuses, God's love will heal and restore all that was lost" (*Imagine the God of Heaven*, pages 68–69). Pastor and theologian Tim Keller echoes this theme, writing, "Our choices have consequences and we are never forced by God to do anything other than what we want. Yet God works out his will perfectly through our willing actions. It is a marvel!"[8]

- *In what ways have you experienced God's healing and restoration for your off-script choices?*

- *How have you seen God work out his will perfectly through your willing choices to love, obey, and commit yourself to him?*

RESPOND

God is sovereign, yet he respects us so much he gave us free will. God gave us free will, yet he is sovereign so he can make something right even out of our wrong choices. The apostle Paul affirms this: "And we know that God causes everything to work together for the good of those who love God and are called according to his purpose for them" (Romans 8:28). Share with God the ways in which you need him to be sovereign over the consequences of your choices—to redeem or heal whatever needs to be made right. Ask him to help you choose life and blessings this day and every day.

PARENT, FRIEND, AND LOVER

"There is no one who loves you more, understands you better, or believes in you more than God. That's why the Bible uses every relational metaphor to describe the incredible love, compassion, and understanding God has toward you. Three of the most prominent metaphors the Bible uses for God are *parent, friend,* and *lover*. As you see how intimately God understands you and the compassion he feels for you, imagine how this could change the way you relate to him." *Imagine the God of Heaven*, page 83

READ

> When Israel was a child, I loved him,
>   and I called my son out of Egypt.
> But the more I called to him,
>   the farther he moved from me. . . .
> I myself taught Israel how to walk,
>   leading him along by the hand.
> But he doesn't know or even care
>   that it was I who took care of him. . . .
>   I myself stooped to feed him.
> HOSEA 11:1-4

I am the one who answers your prayers and cares for you.
HOSEA 14:8

> "When that day comes," says the LORD,
>   "you will call me 'my husband'
>   instead of 'my master.'. . .

I will make you my wife forever,
    showing you righteousness and justice,
    unfailing love and compassion.
I will be faithful to you and make you mine,
    and you will finally know me as the LORD."
HOSEA 2:16, 19-20

REFLECT

1. In the Hosea passages (and throughout the Bible), God is
   described as a parent, friend, and lover.

   - *Which of these metaphors best describes the way you generally
     relate to God?*

   - *Which makes you the most uncomfortable? Why?*

   - *Keeping in mind the relational metaphor that makes you
     uncomfortable, in what ways might your understanding of God
     and your relationship with God need to grow to help you love
     God more?*

2. People often develop their ideas about God from what one or both of their parents or caregivers were like.

- *Complete the following statement: "Based on how I grew up, the three words or phrases I would use to describe my parents are . . ."*

- *In what ways, if any, have these same three words or phrases characterized your understanding of your relationship with God over the years?*

- *Be assured, God is a perfect parent who has love and compassion for you and wants to provide for you and guide you with his omniscient, inerrant wisdom. In what ways, if any, do you want to relate to God differently than you do or did to your own parents or caregivers?*

3. Jesus said, "I no longer call you slaves, because a master doesn't confide in his slaves. Now you are my friends" (John 15:15).

- *What three to five words or phrases would you use to describe a master/slave relationship?*

- *What three to five words or phrases would you use to describe a good friendship?*

- *In what ways, if any, does your relationship with God resemble a master/slave relationship? A good friendship?*

- *How has the quality of your friendship with God impacted how you do life with him? Your ability to trust him? Your desire to tell others about him?*

4. Characteristics of a relationship between lovers might include tenderness, intimacy, ecstasy, and oneness. In what ways have you experienced these in your relationship with God?

RESPOND

You have a God who wants to parent you through life, to be your best friend, and to have an intimate oneness with you typically only experienced by lovers. That is something worth celebrating! Thank God for the relationship you have with him and ask him to help you experience his love in all of these ways in the days ahead.

DAY 5

YOU ARE WITNESSES

The book *I Once Was Dead* tells the story of Swidiq[9] Kanana, who grew up the son of a Muslim sheik in Rwanda. Swidiq had an NDE in which, to his surprise, he met Jesus. He says Jesus told him, "I died for man. And you are among those I died for. Do not deny it again. You must tell others. Reveal it."[10]

Swidiq returned to his body during his own burial service. He pulled a sheet off his face, climbed off the table, and stared, shocked to see several men with shovels standing around a six-foot hole. "He had been dead for over twelve hours, and a large gathering of Muslims was about to lay him in the grave. Swidiq recalls, 'I began shouting, "Jesus is here! Jesus is here! . . . He brought me back! It was Jesus who got me and brought me back!"' That was too much for this crowd of terrified Muslims. They began running hysterically in all directions.[11]

"Swidiq became a follower of Jesus, and eventually an Anglican priest" (*Imagine the God of Heaven*, page 112). God rescued him from many attempts on his life after he left Islam.

READ

Then [Jesus] said, "When I was with you before, I told you that everything written about me in the law of Moses and the prophets and in the Psalms must be fulfilled." Then he opened their minds to understand the Scriptures. And he said, "Yes, it was written long ago that the Messiah would suffer and die and rise from the dead on the third day. It was also written that this message would be proclaimed in the authority of his name to all the nations, beginning in Jerusalem: 'There is forgiveness of sins for all who repent.' You are witnesses of all these things.

  "And now I will send the Holy Spirit, just as my Father

promised. But stay here in the city until the Holy Spirit comes and fills you with power from heaven."

LUKE 24:44-49

But you will receive power when the Holy Spirit comes upon you. And you will be my witnesses, telling people about me everywhere—in Jerusalem, throughout Judea, in Samaria, and to the ends of the earth.

ACTS 1:8

REFLECT

1. Swidiq Kanana's story is a dramatic one in which he was simultaneously saved from physical and spiritual death. And his elation at being saved knew no bounds—he shouted with joy that Jesus had saved him. Even if your story of coming to faith isn't as dramatic as Swidiq's, you, too, were saved from death when you accepted Christ.

   - *How did you respond on the day you accepted Christ? For example, what emotions did you feel? How excited and willing were you to share your newfound faith with others?*

   - *How has God declaring you not guilty and releasing you from the death penalty impacted your life? In what ways has the joy of your salvation increased, decreased, or changed? Has the excitement of letting others know what you found increased or decreased? Why?*

- *God is a God of justice, and justice demands punishment for wrongdoing. The Bible tells us "all have sinned" (Romans 3:23, NIV) and deserve God's justice. But when we turn to God because of faith in Jesus and what he did on the cross, we are forgiven and freed from condemnation and the power of sin. We read in Romans 8:1-2, "So now there is no condemnation for those who belong to Christ Jesus. And because you belong to him, the power of the life-giving Spirit has freed you from the power of sin that leads to death." Do you live free from condemnation? If not, why not?*

3. In Luke 24, Jesus said that we must proclaim the message that forgiveness of sins is available to everyone. Everyone needs to hear this good news! What is your experience of sharing the good news with others?

4. Jesus said the Holy Spirit gives us power to be his witnesses. Most of our excuses for not sharing our faith—such as "I wouldn't be good at it," "I don't know what to say," or "I couldn't answer their questions"—are focused on "I." However, our success in sharing our faith is not found in us but in the Holy Spirit empowering us to care about others as he does.

- *What fears or excuses, if any, tend to keep you from sharing your faith with others?*

- *How might you overcome those fears or excuses by imagining yourself in partnership with the Holy Spirit? For example, you can declare, "I may not know what to say now, but with the power of the Holy Spirit, I can learn." Or, "With the power of the Holy Spirit, I can help someone find answers to their questions."*

5. Who are three people God has put in your life who—as far as you know—don't know of God's great love for them or of his forgiveness offered in Christ?

- *Commit to praying for each of these three people.*
- *Circle the name of the person with whom you'd feel the most comfortable having a spiritual conversation. Look for an opportunity to ask that person about their spiritual beliefs this week. Simply asking questions and listening well can lead to opportunities to share the good news of Christ with others.*

RESPOND

Thank God that he loves and values your life so much that there's nothing he hasn't given for you to set you free of all fear and all condemnation! And thank him for the privilege of partnering with his Holy Spirit to help others know that he wants this freedom for them because he loves them the same.

THE GOD OF COMPASSION

OPEN

In *The Lion King* there's a great line about leadership and compassion. The lioness Sarabi scolds Scar, also a lion and the animated film's main antagonist, with the words, "Scar, a true king's power is his compassion."[12]

The Latin roots of the word *compassion* literally mean to "suffer with." Compassion is generally understood as a feeling we have when confronted with and concerned about the suffering of others, which then leads us to take action to relieve that suffering.

Scar no doubt felt that the power of kings put them above suffering or feeling pity and therefore that compassion was either beneath them or a sign of weakness. He was wrong.

Questions

1. In what ways might compassion make a king or any leader more powerful in the ways that matter most?

2. Briefly recall a time when you were the recipient of compassion. How were you hurting, and what led the other person to notice? How did that person's compassionate response impact you?

3. When have you recently shown compassion to someone? How were they suffering, and what led you notice? What action did you take to help or to ease their pain?

READ

As you read the following stories that highlight Jesus' compassion, take note of what he saw, what he felt, and what he did.

> Jesus traveled through all the towns and villages of that area, teaching in the synagogues and announcing the Good News about the Kingdom. And he healed every kind of disease and illness. When he saw the crowds, he had compassion on them because they were confused and helpless, like sheep without a shepherd. He said to his disciples, "The harvest is great, but the workers are few. So pray to the Lord who is in charge of the harvest; ask him to send more workers into his fields."
>
> MATTHEW 9:35-38

> As soon as Jesus heard the news, he left in a boat to a remote area to be alone. But the crowds heard where he was headed and followed on foot from many towns. Jesus saw the huge crowd as he stepped from the boat, and he had compassion on them and healed their sick.
>
> That evening the disciples came to him and said, "This is a remote place, and it's already getting late. Send the crowds away so they can go to the villages and buy food for themselves."

But Jesus said, "That isn't necessary—you feed them."

"But we have only five loaves of bread and two fish!" they answered.

"Bring them here," he said. Then he told the people to sit down on the grass. Jesus took the five loaves and two fish, looked up toward heaven, and blessed them. Then, breaking the loaves into pieces, he gave the bread to the disciples, who distributed it to the people. They all ate as much as they wanted, and afterward, the disciples picked up twelve baskets of leftovers. About 5,000 men were fed that day, in addition to all the women and children!

MATTHEW 14:13-21

Soon afterward Jesus went with his disciples to the village of Nain, and a large crowd followed him. A funeral procession was coming out as he approached the village gate. The young man who had died was a widow's only son, and a large crowd from the village was with her. When the Lord saw her, his heart overflowed with compassion. "Don't cry!" he said. Then he walked over to the coffin and touched it, and the bearers stopped. "Young man," he said, "I tell you, get up." Then the dead boy sat up and began to talk! And Jesus gave him back to his mother.

Great fear swept the crowd, and they praised God, saying, "A mighty prophet has risen among us," and "God has visited his people today." And the news about Jesus spread throughout Judea and the surrounding countryside.

LUKE 7:11-17

In these stories, we witness the power of King Jesus' compassion and how it changed the lives of those he encountered. It should lead us to be grateful that he has that same compassion for us and inspire us to have that same compassion for others.

Questions

1. Hungry people, diseases, and funeral processions were ordinary occurrences, yet Jesus had extraordinary responses.

    • *What stood out most to you about what Jesus saw, what he felt, and what he did in response to the suffering he encountered?*

    • *In the three stories, Jesus had compassion on those suffering physical illness, spiritual confusion and helplessness, physical hunger, and emotional pain. Which of these or other kinds of needs are most likely to move you with compassion? Which are least likely to move you with compassion? Share the reasons for your response.*

2. Which of the following statements best describes why you sometimes struggle to feel or act with compassion when you encounter someone in need?

    • *"There are too many hurting people, and nothing I could do would make a difference."*

    • *"I'm too busy right now with my own responsibilities. I'll try to do something later."*

    • *"There are already people who are helping with that."*

    • *"I don't think I have anything to offer."*

- *"Whatever they're going through is probably their fault. And besides, I don't like drama."*

- *Other:*

3. In each story, Jesus' compassion led him to take action—he prayed, asked others to pray, touched and healed the sick, fed the hungry, and spoke words of life and truth.

    - *What do these examples reveal about the heart and character of God?*

    - *How does imagining God as compassionate affect how you relate to him?*

WATCH

Watch the Session 3 video and take notes on your reflections and questions.

"All love involves risk—love can be rejected—and humanity keeps rejecting God's love, and yet he won't give up. He keeps pursuing us."

"Don't ever believe the lie that God doesn't understand you—or doesn't care for you, won't forgive you, or has even turned his back on you. It's not true."

"Is it difficult or easy for you to believe that God has compassion for you and wants the best for you? Why or why not?"

DISCUSS

1. If what the people on the video said about God is true, how might it change or deepen how you relate to God?

2. In *Imagine the God of Heaven*, we read of Santosh Acharjee, who went into cardiac arrest and then died. He had a NDE in which he described feeling loved by God and safe. He said, "What was the reason for His grace upon me? I did not do anything special to deserve His Mercy. Yet, I felt all along that He loved me. He showed His Compassion to me. . . . Relentlessly, I prayed for His Guidance and asked Him to show me the Truth and the Way. And He did! He answered all my prayers. Thankfully, I found the Light that I was looking for, and, gradually, I found the meaning of everything that I witnessed and much

more. Through His Grace, I found my true identity in Him"[13] (pages 81–82).

- Based on what you read in the book or watched on the video, what stands out most to you about the NDErs' experiences of God's compassion or other characteristics?

- In what ways, if any, do you relate to the NDErs' experiences of God's love and compassion? How has God shown his compassion to you?

- Santosh made a fascinating connection between experiencing God's compassion and finding his true identity. Why might experiencing God's compassion be a key to finding our true identity in him?

3. God is a God of justice, which means he cannot let sin go unpunished. And yet he still loves us and wants to have a relationship with us. That's why Jesus went to the cross. His sacrifice satisfied God's justice and made a way for us to have a relationship with God.

- In what ways might the cross be the ultimate example of Jesus' compassion?

- *If you've accepted Christ, how has experiencing God's forgiveness changed how you relate to God? How do you understand the connection between God's justice, his compassion, and his forgiveness?*

4. When Dr. Mary Neal encountered Jesus in her NDE, she said, "He looked like bottomless kindness and compassion"[14] (*Imagine the God of Heaven*, page 82).

    - *In what ways, if any, might your relationship with Jesus change if you were to take seriously this statement—that he is bottomless kindness and compassion? For example, consider how it might change things such as your experience of prayer, worship, reading Scripture, and spending time alone with God.*

    - *How might believing Jesus is bottomless kindness and compassion impact your ability to treat others with compassion?*

5. Because of Jesus' compassion, the author of Hebrews writes that we can "come boldly to the throne of our gracious God. There we will receive his mercy, and we will find grace to help us when we need it most" (Hebrews 4:16).

- *For what struggle or circumstance are you most in need of grace, mercy, and help right now?*

- *Is there anything that might keep you from boldly approaching God to ask for what you need? What would that be and why?*

CLOSE
Encouragement

The example of Jesus and the experiences of NDErs provide a powerful reminder that God is "the Father of compassion and the God of all comfort, who comforts us in all our troubles, so that we can comfort those in any trouble with the comfort we ourselves receive from God" (2 Corinthians 1:3-4, NIV).

Prayer

> *Boldly take your troubles to God to receive his comfort, mercy, and help. Ask him to help you extend his compassion to the hurting people he puts in your path this week.*

 This coming week: Read chapters 8–11 of *Imagine the God of Heaven* and complete the personal studies.

THE ETERNAL DANCE

In chapter 8 of *Imagine the God of Heaven*, we read about the mystery of the Trinity and hear from Heidi, Crystal, Dean, and Bill, each of whom had NDEs in which they experienced God the Father, God the Son, *and* God the Holy Spirit. Each person also clearly understood that the Father, Son, and Holy Spirit exist as one God.

Theologians use the word *Trinity* (which comes from Latin and means "three" or "triad") to describe God's unique three-in-one, one-yet-three relationship. In the 700s CE, a theologian named John of Damascus used the Greek word *perichoresis* to explain the trinitarian nature of God. *Peri* means "around" and *choresis* comes from the Greek verb *chōreō*, meaning "to go," "to come," or "to be in motion." *Perichoresis* essentially means "to move around," "to move through," or "to encircle." The three persons of the Trinity are in a continual dance with one another. They move in perfect unison, and it's hard to tell where one ends and the other begins.

John Burke writes, "God is one God in three persons. That revelation makes sense when we remember that God *is* love. Yet, love is always relational. So, before God created anything, whom did God love? The answer is found in the persons of God: The Father loves the Son loves the Holy Spirit loves the Father. God *is* a relationship. The Creator of everything is a relationship of love" (*Imagine the God of Heaven*, pages 146–147).

READ

Jesus affirmed there is only one God but also acknowledged the mystery of the Trinity when he said:

> The Scriptures say, "You must worship the LORD your God and serve only him."
> LUKE 4:8

And this is the way to have eternal life—to know you, the
only true God, and Jesus Christ, the one you sent to earth. . . .
I pray that they will all be one, just as you and I are one—as
you are in me, Father, and I am in you. And may they be in us
so that the world will believe you sent me.
JOHN 17:3, 21

God pointed people to Jesus when he said:

This is my dearly loved Son, who brings me great joy. Listen
to him.
MATTHEW 17:5

Jesus pointed people to the Father when he said:

My Father is always working. . . . I tell you the truth, the
Son can do nothing by himself. He does only what he
sees the Father doing. Whatever the Father does, the Son
also does.
JOHN 5:17, 19

I don't speak on my own authority. The Father who sent me
has commanded me what to say and how to say it.
JOHN 12:49

The Holy Spirit pointed people to Jesus, and Jesus pointed people to
the Holy Spirit when he said:

The Spirit . . . will come to you from the Father and will testify
all about me.
JOHN 15:26

He will bring me glory by telling you whatever he receives
from me.
JOHN 16:14

REFLECT

1. How is the idea of *perichoresis* evident in the verses you read about God the Father, God the Son, and God the Holy Spirit? In other words, how might their relationship with each other resemble a dance?

2. If God lives in eternal community and we are created in God's image, what does that suggest about what it means to be fully human? To relate to God and others?

3. What do you learn about loving relationships when you realize that God *is* a loving relationship? How does that impact the way you view your relationships?

4. Jesus makes a startling statement when he prays that we, his followers, would be one just as he and God are one, and that we can be "in" God, participants in the dance of the Trinity.

- *Why do you think it's so important that Jesus' followers be united in a way that reflects the Trinity?*

- *In what ways, if any, have you experienced this kind of oneness with other Christians? With God?*

- *What changes could you make to help you live more in loving, unified relationships with others? Are there any broken relationships that need repair?*

5. Jesus says that if we are one with each other as he and the Father are one, and if we are one with God, then the world will believe God sent him (see John 17:21). Why do you think living in authentic community with other believers and with God is the greatest evidence for nonbelievers that God is real and that he truly sent Jesus?

RESPOND

Praise God that he lives in an eternal community of love and thank him for inviting you into his community. Ask him to help you experience it more and more.

DIVINE POWER

God the Father is almighty and glorious. Father Cedric Pisegna recalls feeling overwhelmed by the glory of God in his NDE: "I was standing before the throne of God! I was experiencing the pleasure all humans seek all our lives, the joy for which we were made. God's presence is the ultimate pleasure for which we long. . . . What I encountered when I stood before God was glorious and electric. I wasn't allowed to see a form, but what I did see was light. It was as if I were looking at the sun with my eyes closed, yet even more luminescent. Psalm 104:1-2 tells us the truth that God is 'clothed with honor and majesty, and covers himself with light as with a garment.' I didn't just see the light, the brightness embraced me. The light was somehow alive. In addition to the brightness, there was an overwhelming glory. . . . God's glory is not just something I observed, it was an electricity and ecstasy that I felt. It was a rhythmic powerful surge that ran all through me"[15] (*Imagine the God of Heaven*, page 161).

READ

> Yours, O LORD, is the greatness, the power, the glory, the victory, and the majesty. Everything in the heavens and on earth is yours, O LORD, and this is your kingdom. We adore you as the one who is over all things. Wealth and honor come from you alone, for you rule over everything. Power and might are in your hand, and at your discretion people are made great and given strength.
>
> 1 CHRONICLES 29:11-12

I also pray that you will understand the incredible greatness of God's power for us who believe him. This is the same mighty power that raised Christ from the dead and seated him in the place of honor at God's right hand in the heavenly realms. Now he is far above any ruler or authority or power or leader or anything else—not only in this world but also in the world to come.

EPHESIANS 1:19-21

By his divine power, God has given us everything we need for living a godly life. We have received all of this by coming to know him, the one who called us to himself by means of his marvelous glory and excellence. And because of his glory and excellence, he has given us great and precious promises. These are the promises that enable you to share his divine nature and escape the world's corruption caused by human desires.

2 PETER 1:3-4

REFLECT

1. What do you learn about God from David's prayer in 1 Chronicles 29:11-12?

2. In what ways have you seen or experienced God's power? Consider examples from the Bible and nature as well as your own life and the lives of others.

3. What, if anything, sometimes makes you question or doubt God's power? In what ways, if any, does what you've learned about God from Scripture and NDE testimonies help you with your questions or doubts?

4. In the Ephesians passage, the apostle Paul makes a stunning claim—that God's power, the same power that raised Jesus from the dead, is available to those who believe in him. Mark an *X* on the continuums below to indicate your response to each of the statements about your experience of God's power.

I feel God's power at work in me . . .

Never   Rarely   Occasionally   Frequently   Always

I recognize God's power at work in the world around me and in the lives of others . . .

Never   Rarely   Occasionally   Frequently   Always

Briefly describe the reasons for your responses.

5. God said to the apostle Paul, "My power works best in weakness" (2 Corinthians 12:9). This implies that we may not *feel* powerful but rather weak when God's power is at work.

   - *Where are you weak and therefore perfectly situated to receive God's power?*

   - *The apostle Paul wrote, "I am glad to boast about my weaknesses, so that the power of Christ can work through me. . . . For when I am weak, then I am strong" (2 Corinthians 12:9, 10). In what ways does this truth challenge you about what it means to experience God's power? In what ways does it encourage you?*

6. We read in 2 Peter that God gives us his power so we can live a godly life. Where do you most need God's power to become more like him right now? Why?

RESPOND

Use David's prayer in 1 Chronicles 29:11-12 as the foundation for your own prayer. Praise God for his power and ask him to help you live in that power more fully this week.

WE HAVE SEEN HIS GLORY

At the beginning of chapter 10 in *Imagine the God of Heaven*, we meet Randy Kay, a CEO whose medical records showed that his heart had stopped beating for thirty minutes. Randy describes the closeness and intimacy he felt with Jesus in his NDE, and how Jesus treated him as a beloved friend.

John Burke writes, "God became one of us! God gets us. He can relate to us in every way. He's like a best friend or devoted older brother—someone in whose presence we can feel so comfortable, so known, so loved, and so understood. No one knows us better. Imagine it! . . . I think that's why NDErs such as Randy and others feel so comfortable and at home with the Lord. He's like a combination of a best friend or a big brother and the wisest, most loving parent, all at the same time" (*Imagine the God of Heaven*, page 174).

READ

The one who is the true light, who gives light to everyone, was coming into the world. . . .

So the Word became human and made his home among us. He was full of unfailing love and faithfulness. And we have seen his glory, the glory of the Father's one and only Son.
JOHN 1:9, 14

Therefore, it was necessary for him [Jesus] to be made in every respect like us, his brothers and sisters, so that he could be our merciful and faithful High Priest before God. Then he could offer a sacrifice that would take away the sins of the people. Since he himself has gone through suffering and testing, he is able to help us when we are being tested.
HEBREWS 2:17-18

Christ is the visible image of the invisible God.
> He existed before anything was created and is supreme over
> all creation. . . .

For God in all his fullness
> was pleased to live in Christ,

and through him God reconciled
> everything to himself.

He made peace with everything in heaven and on earth
> by means of Christ's blood on the cross.

COLOSSIANS 1:15, 19-20

And you are my friends if you do what I command you. I do not call you servants any longer, because servants do not know what their master is doing. Instead, I call you friends, because I have told you everything I heard from my Father.

JOHN 15:14-15, GNT

REFLECT

1. What do you learn about Jesus from these Bible passages?

2. In his time on earth, Jesus was fully God and fully human. How might you explain this truth in terms a ten-year-old would understand? Why is it important to understand?

3. The author of Hebrews writes that Jesus became like us in every way.

   - *Which of the attributes of Christ described in the Scripture passages above is most meaningful and encouraging to you?*

   - *How might meditating on these characteristics of Jesus change the way you pray?*

4. Jesus became like us in every way, except one: "This High Priest of ours understands our weaknesses, for he faced all of the same testings we do, yet he did not sin" (Hebrews 4:15). He lived a human life, experienced the same kinds of temptation and pain you do, and then he died for you. Hebrews 2:17 says Jesus had to become like people to be able to "offer a sacrifice that would take away the sins of the people." Why do you think Jesus had to become human for his sacrifice to count for humans?

5. Jesus described those who follow him as friends. Among other things, friends enjoy spending time together, share common interests, care for each other, listen to each other, trust each

other, honor each other, and are honest and transparent with
each other.

- *When you consider these and all the other things that friendship
  includes, how would you describe what it means that Jesus says
  you can be a friend of his?*

- *What aspects of friendship are you currently experiencing with
  Jesus? What aspects of friendship might you be missing out on or
  want to experience more?*

6. Why do you think Jesus connects friendship with doing what
   he commands? Why would obeying him be the defining
   characteristic of being friends with him?

RESPOND

Briefly identify six to eight attributes of Jesus that are most meaningful
to you. Praise and thank him for each one. Invite him to be a friend
to you in the ways you most need a friend right now. Ask Jesus where
you need to act in faith to obey him so that you can be a better friend
to him.

GOD'S BEST FOR YOU

The Holy Spirit is God. The Holy Spirit is God with us. And for those who have put their faith in Jesus, the Holy Spirit is God *in* us. Jesus said, "I will ask the Father, and he will give you another Advocate, who will never leave you. He is the Holy Spirit, who leads into all truth" (John 14:16-17). The Greek word translated as "Advocate" is *paraklētos.* This word can also be translated as "Comforter," "Counselor," and "Helper." How amazing is that? Jesus promised to send his Spirit—the full essence of the triune God—to be with us always and to be our advocate, comforter, counselor, and helper as we go through life.

READ

I will ask the Father, and he will give you another Advocate, who will never leave you. He is the Holy Spirit, who leads into all truth. The world cannot receive him, because it isn't looking for him and doesn't recognize him. But you know him, because he lives with you now and later will be in you. No, I will not abandon you as orphans—I will come to you. . . . When I am raised to life again, you will know that I am in my Father, and you are in me, and I am in you. . . .

It is best for you that I go away, because if I don't, the Advocate won't come. If I do go away, then I will send him to you.

JOHN 14:16-18, 20; 16:7

Don't you realize that all of you together are the temple of God and that the Spirit of God lives in you?

1 CORINTHIANS 3:16

And do not bring sorrow to God's Holy Spirit by the way you live. Remember, he has identified you as his own, guaranteeing that you will be saved on the day of redemption.
EPHESIANS 4:30

REFLECT

1. Speaking to his disciples, Jesus said that it was best for him to go away so he could send the Holy Spirit. What are some reasons it might be better to have the Holy Spirit with us than to have Jesus with us like he was with the disciples two thousand years ago?

2. Describe how you have experienced the Holy Spirit as your . . .

Advocate

Comforter

Counselor

Helper

4. John Burke writes, "Jesus says the ultimate Counselor, Therapist, and Guide is already with us, ready to help. Do we consult him? Do we seek his guidance? Learning to quiet ourselves and listen for his guidance is the single most important thing we can do. I believe this is what Jesus meant when he said that we will bear spiritual fruit when we remain connected to him, like a branch to a vine. This is the one thing we must do to grow spiritually" (*Imagine the God of Heaven*, page 196).

- *Using the metaphor of a branch and a vine, how would you characterize your connection to Jesus right now?*

- *What spiritual fruit is your connection with Jesus producing? In other words, how are you growing spiritually?*

5. In his letter to the Ephesians, the apostle Paul writes that we must not bring sorrow to the Holy Spirit by the way we live.

- *What about the way you live right now might be bringing the Holy Spirit sorrow?*

- *What about the way you live right now might be bringing the Holy Spirit joy?*

RESPOND

The apostle Paul wrote, "The Spirit helps us in our weakness. We do not know what we ought to pray for, but the Spirit himself intercedes for us through wordless groans" (Romans 8:26, NIV). Thank the Holy Spirit for always being with you, for being available to help and empower you, and for being your prayer partner. Ask the Holy Spirit to pray for you, interceding on your behalf for whatever it is you need to make him joyful by the way you live.

WALK BY THE SPIRIT

God offers us a life-giving and power-supplying connection with him. In John 15:4-5, Jesus called it "abiding" (ESV) or "remaining" in him. The apostle Paul called it "walk[ing] by the Spirit" (Galatians 5:16, NIV). Both abiding with Jesus and walking by the Spirit are invitations to spend each moment doing life with God.

John Burke writes, "Do this one thing—walk by the Spirit daily—and you don't have to white-knuckle in your own effort to 'stop this' or 'try harder' to quit that, or muster up more religious effort to 'be good.' God grows good fruit from within, naturally. It doesn't mean it's always easy, or that there are no struggles, but this one thing is the key to growth. It's a very freeing way of life. . . . No amount of religious 'trying harder' heals us and changes us from within. The Holy Spirit does for us what we cannot do for ourselves" (*Imagine the God of Heaven*, page 197).

READ

So I say, walk by the Spirit, and you will not gratify the desires of the flesh. For the flesh desires what is contrary to the Spirit, and the Spirit what is contrary to the flesh. They are in conflict with each other, so that you are not to do whatever you want. But if you are led by the Spirit, you are not under the law. . . .

But the fruit of the Spirit is love, joy, peace, forbearance, kindness, goodness, faithfulness, gentleness and self-control. Against such things there is no law. Those who belong to Christ Jesus have crucified the flesh with its passions and desires. Since we live by the Spirit, let us keep in step with the Spirit.

GALATIANS 5:16-18, 22-25, NIV

Remain in me, and I will remain in you. For a branch cannot produce fruit if it is severed from the vine, and you cannot be fruitful unless you remain in me. Yes, I am the vine; you are the branches. Those who remain in me, and I in them, will produce much fruit. For apart from me you can do nothing.
JOHN 15:4-5

REFLECT

1. If someone asked you to explain what it looks like to "walk by the Spirit," what would you say? What practical guidance might you give them?

2. How would you explain what it means to "remain" or "abide" in Jesus? How does a person actually do that?

3. Both Bible passages promise that walking by the Spirit and remaining in Jesus produce fruit in our lives, such as growing in godly character—increasing in love, joy, peace, patience, kindness, goodness, faithfulness, gentleness, and self-control. What kind of spiritual fruit do you most want to experience in your life right now? Why?

4. Most people try to change (become more godly) by trying harder. But trying harder rarely produces long-term change and spiritual growth in our lives. At best, it may lead to some short-term behavior modification, and it is not the way of Jesus. Jesus tells us that we grow through our connection to him. When in your life have you felt most connected to God? What do you think led to that deeper sense of connection?

5. Do some brainstorming by making a list of three to five things you could do in the next twenty-four hours to remain in Jesus and walk with the Holy Spirit.

- *Circle one or two of the items on your list and commit to following through on them.*
- *How do you hope your commitment will make a difference and help keep you connected to Jesus throughout the day?*

RESPOND

Thank God that the way you grow spiritually and increase your influence is not by trying harder, which would mean it's up to you, but by abiding in Christ and walking with the Spirit, which means it is up to him.

THE GOD WHO IS ONE YET THREE

OPEN

God is one, yet three. He is three, yet one. God is God the Father, God the Son, and God the Holy Spirit. It is not that God sometimes appears as the Father, sometimes the Son, and other times the Spirit. He is always all three. He is one essence but three persons who live together in such an interdependent, connected community of love that they exist as one God. Although the word *Trinity* does not appear in the Bible, it is the word theologians started using around 200 CE to describe God's three-in-one nature.

In the Old Testament, people experienced God mainly as the Father—the God who is powerful, holy, unseen, somewhat distant due to our sin, and therefore hard to know. In the New Testament, Jesus the Son came to earth, and people experienced God face-to-face and as someone much easier to know. After his death and resurrection, Jesus left the earth and sent the Holy Spirit so that people could experience God *in* them. This progression demonstrates God's increasing engagement and intimacy with his people.

Questions

1. The Trinity can be difficult to understand, but God's revealed nature is also beautiful. What appeals to you or intrigues you about the Trinity?

2. If you grew up in church, how was the Trinity taught? If you did not grow up in church, what was your first impression when you learned about the Trinity?

3. If one of the three persons of the Trinity was emphasized more in your earlier understanding, or another was mostly left out, why do you think that was?

4. If you feel more connected to one member of the Trinity, or struggle more with one, why do you think that is?

READ

All praise to God, the Father of our Lord Jesus Christ, who has blessed us with every spiritual blessing in the heavenly realms because we are united with Christ.

EPHESIANS 1:3

And when you believed in Christ, he identified you as his own by giving you the Holy Spirit, whom he promised long ago. The Spirit is God's guarantee that he will give us the inheritance he promised and that he has purchased us to be his own people. He did this so we would praise and glorify him.
EPHESIANS 1:13-14

But God is so rich in mercy, and he loved us so much, that even though we were dead because of our sins, he gave us life when he raised Christ from the dead.
EPHESIANS 2:4-5

You lived in this world without God and without hope. But now you have been united with Christ Jesus. Once you were far away from God, but now you have been brought near to him through the blood of Christ.

For Christ himself has brought peace to us. He united Jews and Gentiles into one people when, in his own body on the cross, he broke down the wall of hostility that separated us.
EPHESIANS 2:12-14

Now all of us can come to the Father through the same Holy Spirit because of what Christ has done for us.
EPHESIANS 2:18

And the cornerstone is Christ Jesus himself. We are carefully joined together in him, becoming a holy temple for the Lord. Through him you Gentiles are also being made part of this dwelling where God lives by his Spirit.
EPHESIANS 2:20-22

Be filled with the Holy Spirit.
EPHESIANS 5:18

Questions

1. What do these verses reveal about each person of the Trinity and the unique role each plays both in the world and in your life and salvation?

   God the Father

   God the Son

   God the Holy Spirit

2. What in these verses from Ephesians is the most . . .

   Challenging for you to understand?

   Encouraging or exciting?

WATCH

Watch the Session 4 video and take notes on your reflections and questions.

> *"God has been revealing himself as Father, Son, and Spirit since the beginning. From the creation account in Genesis, down through the prophets, God has given us a glimpse of his triune nature, and yet the Bible is also very clear that there are not three gods, but only one true God."*

> *"In heaven, it makes perfect sense that God is one: Father, Son, and Spirit. Here on earth, we still have to grapple with the mystery of it."*

> *"How might understanding God as a divine relationship change the way you interact with God and prioritize other relationships in your life?"*

DISCUSS

1. What thoughts, feelings, or questions did watching the video bring up for you?

2. What was said that enhanced your understanding of God?

3. In what ways did the video make you more excited to know God in an even deeper way, or to experience God in all his fullness someday in heaven?

4. How can understanding God as Father, Son, and Holy Spirit help you to better connect with God? Live your life for him?

CLOSE
Encouragement

You have a God who loves you and wants to have increasing intimacy with you. He is your loving Father, your compassionate Savior, your ever-present Companion and Counselor.

John Burke writes, "You may wonder, as I have, which of the three you should focus on—the Father, Jesus, or the Holy Spirit? To whom should you pray, or does it even matter? Here's my pastoral wisdom: Don't stress about it. God knows our finite nature. Whatever best helps you to connect with and trust God is probably where God would want you to start. But as you grow in faith, stretch your imagination to include interaction with all three persons of the one triune God" (*Imagine the God of Heaven*, page 151–152).

Prayer

> *Ask God to increase your understanding of and experience with him so you can truly know and worship him and help others to know and worship him.*

This coming week: Read chapters 12–14 of *Imagine the God of Heaven* and complete the personal studies. Note that you will complete the book and personal study portion of the course this week in preparation for the Session 5 group study.

WHEN YOU PRAY

"Your prayers matter to God. As I hope you can now imagine, God is with you always. He is infinite Spirit, so time and distance do not limit God as they do humanity. NDErs attest to this. God not only attends to every single prayer of every person; God answers our prayers in such a way that the outcome works together for our good *and* for the good of all those who love him. Scripture assures us and NDErs testify that in God's presence, all things work together, and it all makes sense.

"I find it encouraging to know that we don't even have to 'do it right' for God to hear or answer our prayers. Prayer is not a puzzle or a formula, something we have to figure out with precision before God will hear us or give us what we ask for. Prayer is simply communicating with God—silently in our hearts or out loud. In prayer, we have a conversation with God, our Creator, who loves us and wants to guide us through life by his Holy Spirit. We don't have to be good at prayer, we simply have to be willing to do it! God promises his Holy Spirit will help us—aligning our will to God's will as he works all things together for good." *Imagine the God of Heaven*, page 216

READ

But when you pray, go away by yourself, shut the door behind you, and pray to your Father in private. Then your Father, who sees everything, will reward you.

When you pray, don't babble on and on as the Gentiles do. They think their prayers are answered merely by repeating their words again and again. Don't be like them, for your Father knows exactly what you need even before you ask him! Pray like this:

Our Father in heaven,
    may your name be kept holy.

May your Kingdom come soon.
May your will be done on earth,
    as it is in heaven.
Give us today the food we need,
and forgive us our sins,
    as we have forgiven those who sin against us.
And don't let us yield to temptation,
    but rescue us from the evil one.

MATTHEW 6:6-13

REFLECT

1. How were you taught to pray when you were a child? For example, when and where did you pray? Did you bow your head, kneel, fold your hands? Did you read prayers, memorize prayers, pray extemporaneously?

2. What does your practice of prayer look like today? In what ways is it similar to or different from the way you prayed as a child?

3. What aspects of prayer do you find most challenging? Why?

4. The Lord's Prayer is a model and an outline we can follow as we learn to communicate with God heart-to-heart. Use the following prompts from the Lord's Prayer as a guide for your own prayer. As you pray, reflect on all you've been learning about God's character.

- *"Our Father in heaven, may your name be kept holy."*

  Honor and worship God for who he is—your heavenly Father.

- *"May your Kingdom come soon."*

  Jesus came to bring God's Kingdom (where God's will and ways are done) to earth. As his followers, we are to be Kingdom people who are establishing his Kingdom. Ask God how you might bring his Kingdom to earth this day.

- *"May your will be done on earth, as it is in heaven."*

  Jesus said, "I have come to do your will" (Hebrews 10:9). Surrender your will to God's will. Ask God to show you how to do his will in all your interactions today. You may even pray through your day, imagining what it might look like to do God's will in each situation.

- *"Give us today the food we need."*

  Acknowledge that God is the giver of all good things (see James 1:17) and ask him to provide for your needs. Remember, God is not stingy, and you can ask him for anything.

- *"And forgive us our sins, as we have forgiven those who sin against us."*

  Invite God to search your heart (see Psalm 139:23-24) and show you where you may be outside his will and therefore need to confess and repent. Admit your sins or wrongs to God, who eternally forgives you in Christ (remember God's promise in 1 John 1:9 that he is faithful to forgive). Because God has forgiven you, ask God to help you do the same for those you need to forgive.

- *"And don't let us yield to temptation, but rescue us from the evil one."*

  We live in a world filled with temptation, and we have a spiritual enemy, but we don't want to sin. Ask God to give you wisdom and the strength you need to resist temptation, especially when you feel weak.

5. Briefly review what you wrote in response to each of the prompts from the Lord's Prayer.

   - *What word or phrase (from what you wrote or from the Lord's Prayer itself) stands out most to you?*

   - *Craft the word or phrase you identified into a one-sentence prayer that you can pray all throughout the day as a way of staying connected to God and aligning your will with his will.*

RESPOND

Think about it: The eternal and sovereign God wants you to talk to him about everything! He is always ready to listen, and he longs for you to experience his presence, peace, and power through prayer. That is something to celebrate!

UNCEASING CONVERSATION

"Unceasing prayer is how we walk through life with the Holy Spirit moment by moment, day by day. We begin as we wake up in the morning and then continue until we go to bed at night, discussing with God every thought, every decision, every event, and every meeting or encounter that comes our way. That's God's desire—that we talk everything over with him, we thank him along the way, and we listen for his guidance through the Holy Spirit's promptings. Unceasing prayer is how we stay connected to God. . . .

"This is the *one thing* Jesus said we must do, and it's really the *only thing* we have to do to become all God intended. When we practice unceasing prayer, staying connected to God's Spirit with a willingness to obey every prompting, Jesus says we will 'bear much fruit' (John 15:5, NIV). The challenge is, most of us have developed the habit of ignoring God most of the day. From the moment we wake up, all we're thinking about is, 'What do *I* have to do today?' 'How do *I* get *my will* done in all things?' So we must develop new habits to help us remain in constant connection with God's Spirit, willing to do his will." *Imagine the God of Heaven*, page 226

READ

> Rejoice always, pray continually, give thanks in all
> circumstances; for this is God's will for you in Christ Jesus.
> 1 THESSALONIANS 5:16-18, NIV

> Don't worry about anything; instead, pray about everything.
> Tell God what you need, and thank him for all he has done.
> Then you will experience God's peace, which exceeds anything
> we can understand. His peace will guard your hearts and
> minds as you live in Christ Jesus.

And now, dear brothers and sisters, one final thing. Fix your thoughts on what is true, and honorable, and right, and pure, and lovely, and admirable. Think about things that are excellent and worthy of praise. Keep putting into practice all you learned and received from me—everything you heard from me and saw me doing. Then the God of peace will be with you.
PHILIPPIANS 4:6-9

Pray in the Spirit at all times and on every occasion. Stay alert and be persistent in your prayers for all believers everywhere.
EPHESIANS 6:18

REFLECT

1. Briefly reflect on your experience of prayer.

   • *How have you experienced God and intimacy with him in prayer?*

   • *Do you think about prayer more as an ongoing conversation with a friend or more as a formal thing you must do a certain way? What or who most shaped your view and practice of prayer?*

   • *The Bible verses today said we are to pray continually, persistently, and about everything. Which of these three, if any, comes most naturally to you? Which do you find most challenging? Why?*

2. God doesn't mean for prayer to be something we do occasionally or once a week at church, but to be an unceasing conversation that helps us do life with him from one moment to the next. Overall, how would you characterize your practice of unceasing prayer right now?

Mark an X on the continuum to indicate your response.

I never pray throughout the day.	I occasionally pray throughout the day.	I always pray throughout the day.

3. In the Philippians passage, Paul stated that praying "about everything" enables us to experience God's peace, which has the power to guard our hearts. The Greek word translated "guard" is *phroureō*. It is a military term, one Paul also used literally in his second letter to the church at Corinth when he wrote, "the governor under King Aretas *guarded* [*phroureō*] the city of Damascus" (2 Corinthians 11:32, NRSVue, emphasis added). To guard in this way is to post sentries who keep watch for threats or enemies.[16]

   • *If God's peace guards our hearts, what might that suggest about the state of our hearts when we're preoccupied with worry?*

- *If God were to post sentries to guard your heart, what enemies would they need to keep watch for? In other words, what worries or anxieties pose the greatest threat to your peace throughout your day? How might unceasing prayer help you against these enemies?*

4. In Ephesians 6:18, Paul wrote that we are to "stay alert and be persistent" in prayer. To be alert is to be watchful, attentive, and ready. To be persistent is to be resolute, steadfast, and determined.

- *Briefly identify a circumstance that required you to be both alert and persistent. For example, it might have been a work task, caring for a child or someone who was ill, learning a new skill, or overcoming an obstacle. What habits of thought and behavior did you develop that enabled you to be alert and persistent in that context?*

- *What insights does that experience provide about what being alert and persistent in prayer might look like for you?*

5. Although the prospect of unceasing prayer may feel overwhelming, it *is* possible to grow in the practice of conversation with God throughout your day—and it is essential for staying connected to God's Spirit and doing life with him. If you believed that it really is possible for you to have an unceasing conversation with God, how do you imagine your life might change by putting this into practice? As a starting point, consider each of the areas listed below.

Mental and emotional health

Physical health

Spiritual health

Relationships

Daily tasks, school, or job

Other:

6. Developing any new skill or habit requires a willingness to fail and try again. It's like learning to walk—and toddlers fall a lot when they're taking their first steps. Accepting that failure is part of the process is how we "fail forward," learning new things from each attempt and applying those lessons to the next attempt. What might it mean for you to fail forward in learning to have an unceasing conversation with God?

7. In the Philippians passage, Paul encouraged his readers to "keep putting into practice all you learned and received." Jesus said, "Everyone who hears these words of mine and puts them into practice is like a wise man who built his house on the rock" (Matthew 7:24, NIV). Jesus also said, "When you obey my commandments, you remain in my love, just as I obey my Father's commandments and remain in his love" (John 15:10).

How might putting unceasing prayer into practice help you to more faithfully obey God's commands? To remain in God's love?

RESPOND

In *Imagine the God of Heaven*, John Burke describes the "60:60 Experiment," a practice of devoting sixty days to staying connected, moment by moment, in an unceasing conversation with God's Spirit. The experiment consists of setting an alert or reminder on your phone or other electronic device for every sixty minutes during your waking hours for sixty days. At each alert, ask, "Lord, how did I do staying connected to you this last hour? How can I remain in your love right now? How well did I let you in on my thoughts, decisions, and interactions? Is there anything you want me to do right now?"

Would you be willing to try it? The 60:60 Experiment could create a new habit that absolutely revolutionizes your life!

NO MATTER HOW AWFUL IT FEELS

"Can you imagine a God who is present with you always, sustaining everything, yet also infinitely beyond all he's created? God's overarching power has no comparison, yet this supreme power is used only in love. . . .

"[God] loves and cares for you, knows you perfectly, and is able to do anything necessary for your ultimate well-being. This truth can give you great reassurance and confidence when life feels chaotic or uncertain. God is infinitely greater than all your problems, troubles, trials, and tribulations. He is with you, and he cares for you, so you can trust that you're going to be okay in his mighty hands." *Imagine the God of Heaven*, page 168

An NDEr named Penny says, "The thing I learned there [in God's presence] is [that] we have this really screwed up view of good and bad. To us, 'good' is when nothing is wrong. 'Bad' is when it doesn't go our way. In the spiritual realm, good is forward motion. No matter how awful it feels. If you're moving forward, growing, positively affecting the lives of other people—even if you're doing it through grief or trials—if you're still doing good work, you're moving forward and it's good. But the day you stop interacting with the world and you're only doing what makes you comfortable—that's bad, even though nothing bad is happening. That's not what we're on earth for"[17] (*Imagine the God of Heaven*, pages 190–191).

READ

Therefore, since we have been made right in God's sight by faith, we have peace with God because of what Jesus Christ our Lord has done for us. Because of our faith, Christ has brought us into this place of undeserved privilege where we now stand, and we confidently and joyfully look forward to sharing God's glory.

We can rejoice, too, when we run into problems and trials,

for we know that they help us develop endurance. And endurance develops strength of character, and character strengthens our confident hope of salvation. And this hope will not lead to disappointment. For we know how dearly God loves us, because he has given us the Holy Spirit to fill our hearts with his love.

ROMANS 5:1-5

Dear brothers and sisters, when troubles of any kind come your way, consider it an opportunity for great joy. For you know that when your faith is tested, your endurance has a chance to grow. So let it grow, for when your endurance is fully developed, you will be perfect and complete, needing nothing.

JAMES 1:2-4

REFLECT

1. Briefly recall some of the trials you have experienced recently or in the past. Overall, would you say your trials drew you closer to God or pushed you farther away from him? Did they increase your faith or lead you to doubt? Why?

2. The passages from Romans and James describe how God wants to do something in us through our trials and demonstrate that trials are a source of faith and character development. In what ways, if any, did you experience this in the trials you identified above?

3. Both passages note the importance of endurance. Commenting on the meaning and significance of endurance, one Bible scholar writes, "Believers do not take the pressure of tribulation passively by abjectly giving in to it; rather, they resist it, like Christ who 'endured' the cross and thus triumphed over suffering."[18]

   - To "resist" is to counteract, to oppose, or to act in opposition. How does this inform your understanding of what endurance is and why it's so important for us to develop?

   - What might it mean in practical terms to "resist" in your trials and hardships?

   - How does endurance or resistance connect to Paul's description of "confident hope" and James's description of being made "perfect and complete"?

4. In describing her NDE, Penny said she learned to think differently about what is "good" and "bad." She said, "Good is . . . moving forward, growing, positively affecting the lives of other people—even if you're doing it through grief or trials."

- *Using Penny's definition, what "good" might you recognize in your current trials or hardships?*

- *What parallels might there be between what Penny said and the apostle Paul's statement, "And we know that God causes everything to work together for the good of those who love God and are called according to his purpose for them" (Romans 8:28)?*

RESPOND

Take a moment to remember what God has already done *for* you because of your faith in Jesus, and to consider what God will do *in* you through your trials. Ask him to help you develop endurance and to keep moving forward even in your hardships. Ask him to fill your heart with his love.

THE GOD OF ALL JOY

"There is one attribute of God often overlooked by theologians, miscalculated by most people, yet clearly revealed in Scripture—God's eternal joy! Failing to imagine God as the source of all our joy and laughter, fun and games, pleasures and enjoyments of life has led many people to turn away from God. But we should be running toward God if we desire to enjoy life fully! As one of my favorite authors C. S. Lewis declared, 'Joy is the serious business of Heaven.'"[19] *Imagine the God of Heaven*, page 259

One NDEr who agrees is Rebecca Springer, who lived in the late 1800s. John Burke writes, "Rebecca's experience more than a century ago confirms many of the common experiences of heaven I've heard NDErs relay today. What marks Rebecca's NDE are the varied joys of heaven she experienced, which remind us that God is the God of all joy. . . . Rebecca later reflected that compared to earth's joys, 'there is a depth, a mystery to all that pertains to the divine life, which I dare not try to describe. . . . Suffice it to say, that no joy we know on earth, however rare, however sacred, can be more than the faintest shadow of the joy we there find'"[20] (*Imagine the God of Heaven*, pages 254, 259).

READ

And God saw that it was good.
GENESIS 1:10, 12, 18, 21, 25

But be glad and rejoice forever
    in what I will create,
for I will create Jerusalem to be a delight
    and its people a joy.
I will rejoice over Jerusalem
    and take delight in my people;

the sound of weeping and of crying
    will be heard in it no more.
ISAIAH 65:18-19, NIV

For the Lord your God is living among you.
    He is a mighty savior.
He will take delight in you with gladness. . . .
    He will rejoice over you with joyful songs.
ZEPHANIAH 3:17

The joy of the Lord is your strength!
NEHEMIAH 8:10

REFLECT

1. Briefly review the two columns of words.

Joyful	*Joyless*
Cheerful	*Sorrowful*
Enjoyable	*Disagreeable*
Lighthearted	*Stern*
Delighting	*Upset*
Celebratory	*Solemn*

- *People tend to associate God with the words in the column on the right. Why do you think that is?*

- *Overall, which list would you say best characterizes how you tend to think of God? In what ways, if any, has what you've read in Imagine the God of Heaven or watched on the videos impacted your view of God when it comes to joy?*

2. In the creation account, God repeatedly pauses after creating to enjoy the goodness of what he created.

   • *What do you think it is about God that leads him to appreciate and celebrate good things?*

   • *As someone who is created in God's image, how well do you do at stopping to appreciate, celebrate, and be thankful for good in your life? For example, good food, good friends, good times with your family, God's goodness? What could you do to grow to be more like God in this area of gratitude and celebration?*

3. Isaiah 65 and Zephaniah 3 demonstrate that God takes delight in and rejoices over his people—over you.

   • *What makes it difficult or easy to imagine God taking joy in you?*

   • *How might it change your relationship with God if you were able to truly believe he delights in and rejoices over you with singing, as the prophet Zephaniah wrote?*

4. The prophet Nehemiah wrote, "The joy of the Lord is your strength!" (Nehemiah 8:10). The Hebrew word translated "strength" is *maoz*. It means "refuge, stronghold, fortress, place of protection."[21] It is the same word used by King David when he wrote, "The Lord is the *stronghold* [*maoz*] of my life" (Psalm 27:1, NIV, emphasis added), and when he pleaded with God, "Be my rock of *protection* [*maoz*]" (Psalm 31:2, emphasis added).

- *How do you understand the connection between God's joy and God's protection? What enemies might come against us that God's joy could protect us from?*

- *In what ways, if any, have you experienced God's joy as strength or protection in the past?*

- *In what circumstance do you most need the strength and protection of God's joy now?*

RESPOND

God rejoices over you with joyful songs. Why don't you do the same back? Pick a favorite worship song and sing it to God. Ask him to strengthen and protect you with his joy in the days ahead.

JOY RADIATING

"If you follow Jesus, joy is your birthright. You are a child of the king of all joy! Joy is where you are headed, joy is what you'll inherit, joy is the norm, and God's joy is available to you, even now. In fact, you can experience the eternal now of God's joy regardless of trials, through tribulations, no matter what circumstances surround you. As a child of God, joy is available because God is with you, and God *is* joy. . . .

"Happiness comes from happenings—when circumstances go our way—but joy comes from God as we seek his ways. Do you realize that you can choose to seek God's joy, even when circumstances around you are anything but happy? The prophet Habakkuk wrote, 'Even though the fig trees have no blossoms, and there are no grapes on the vines; even though the olive crop fails, and the fields lie empty and barren . . . yet I *will rejoice* in the LORD! I *will be joyful* in the God of my salvation!' (Habakkuk 3:17-18, emphasis added). His external life was falling apart, yet Habakkuk made a choice to seek a joy that comes from God—and so can we. God gives a joy that comes from within, a genuine happiness that no circumstance can take away. But maybe you've never imagined God as very joyful, so you don't really look to God for your joy. NDEs reveal an encouraging truth.

"Derry from Finland recalls sitting with Jesus in a heavenly garden as Jesus looked deep into her eyes. 'The joy radiating from his eyes filled my heart with joy, and the memory of it makes my mind happy now even as I write this.'"[22] *Imagine the God of Heaven*, page 260

READ

> You will fill me with joy in your presence,
> with eternal pleasures at your right hand.
> PSALM 16:11, NIV

Rejoice in the Lord always. I will say it again: Rejoice!
PHILIPPIANS 4:4, NIV

God blesses you who weep now,
for in due time you will laugh.
LUKE 6:21

I have told you these things so that you will be filled with my
joy. Yes, your joy will overflow!
JOHN 15:11

REFLECT

1. Happiness is a good feeling that comes and goes with
   circumstances. Joy is also a good feeling—of happiness and
   peace and contentment—but it is founded in God, not in the
   circumstances of our lives.

   - *When have you experienced a joy that could only come from the
     Lord? What led to it? What did you learn from that experience?*

   - *How would you describe the differences between experiencing
     happiness and experiencing joy?*

2. How do you tend to finish these sentences?

   I'll be happy when . . . .

   I would be happy if . . .

4. Use the following questions to do a brief "joy audit" by reflecting on what robs you of joy and what gives you joy.

- *In the course of a normal day, what tends to rob you of joy— of your peace and contentment in God? Consider the tasks, environments, activities, and relationships that diminish your sense of well-being, peace, and contentment.*

- *In the course of a normal day, what tends to bring you joy? Consider the tasks, environments, activities, and relationships that increase your sense of well-being, peace, and contentment.*

- *Which of the things that increase your joy are tied to circumstances—things that can change and therefore may not always be able to provide you joy?*

- *In all of the things you identified, what might it mean to make God your source of joy? How might you look to God for joy when these circumstances or people let you down?*

RESPOND

Jesus wants us to be filled with his joy and for our joy to be overflowing. Ask him to help you learn what this means by helping you to experience his joy today, even when your circumstances are challenging.

THE GOD WHO DOES LIFE
WITH YOU

OPEN

In *Imagine the God of Heaven*, John Burke shares one of the lowest points of his life. Not knowing what else to do, he prayed every morning, "*God, today I want to do life moment by moment with you, willing to do your will as you guide me*" (page 228). Praying that prayer of daily surrender to do God's will transformed his experience of the trial he was in. It led him to find joy, despite his circumstances, for the first time in a long time.

Questions

1. God desires a moment-by-moment relationship with us, but so many believe it's just about following rules or believing the right things or getting a ticket to go to heaven someday. Why do you think it's so easy for so many to miss the point?

2. John spoke of a willingness to do God's will. How might your life change if you were totally willing to do God's will each moment of the day? Why is this such a struggle for most of us?

3. The promise of Scripture is, "The LORD will guide you always" (Isaiah 58:11, NIV). When have you experienced God guiding you? How have you seen God guiding you even though at the time it didn't feel like he was?

READ

We put no confidence in human effort. . . .

Yes, everything else is worthless when compared with the infinite value of knowing Christ Jesus my Lord. For his sake I have discarded everything else, counting it all as garbage, so that I could gain Christ and become one with him. I no longer count on my own righteousness through obeying the law; rather, I become righteous through faith in Christ. For God's way of making us right with himself depends on faith. I want to know Christ and experience the mighty power that raised him from the dead.

PHILIPPIANS 3:3, 8-10

Always be full of joy in the Lord. I say it again—rejoice! Let everyone see that you are considerate in all you do. Remember, the Lord is coming soon.

Don't worry about anything; instead, pray about everything. Tell God what you need, and thank him for all he has done. Then you will experience God's peace, which exceeds anything we can understand. His peace will guard your hearts and minds as you live in Christ Jesus.

And now, dear brothers and sisters, one final thing. Fix your thoughts on what is true, and honorable, and right, and pure, and lovely, and admirable. Think about things that are excellent

and worthy of praise. Keep putting into practice all you learned and received from me—everything you heard from me and saw me doing. Then the God of peace will be with you.
PHILIPPIANS 4:4-9

Questions

1. What do you think the apostle Paul, who wrote this letter to the church at Philippi, means when he states, "We put no confidence in human effort"? Why might a relationship with God mean you no longer have to rely on yourself?

2. Why is *really* knowing Christ more valuable than anything else?

3. How did the NDE stories you read this week in *Imagine the God of Heaven* help you understand what it might mean to live each day in a relationship of joy with God?

4. As we do life with God, prayer replaces worry and God's peace replaces anxiety. How have you experienced this in your relationship with God?

5. How do you think fixing your thoughts on God and "things that are excellent and worthy of praise" might help you learn to trust God even when life isn't going your way?

WATCH

Watch the Session 5 video and take notes on your reflections and questions.

*"God is the giver of everything we love about this life —
yes, we can abuse his good gifts—but everything good
and enjoyable is here because he made it."*

*"You don't have to wait for heaven to begin to experience
the joys of eternal life with God. Jesus says: 'Now this is
eternal life: that they know you, the only true God, and
Jesus Christ, whom you have sent' (John 17:3, NIV)."*

"How might you experience more of his joy in your life daily?"

DISCUSS

1. What in the video stood out most to you?

2. What questions did the interviews leave you with?

3. How did the interviews enhance your understanding of God's heart for you? Of the joy God has and wants to give to you?

4. What have you learned or realized about God through this study that helps you to imagine him differently? How has it changed the way you seek God and relate to God?

CLOSE
Encouragement

God loves you and wants to do life with you, day by day and moment by moment. He invites you to talk to him all the time and about everything. As you do life with God, you can experience his faithfulness and learn to trust him. You can have joy, even in trials, as he guards your heart and mind with his peace.

Prayer

As you conclude this study, tell God what you've come to realize about his amazing love and wonderous attributes, and ask God to help you continue to grow in your knowledge and experience of the God of heaven.

Facilitator's Guide

THE ROLE OF FACILITATOR is an important responsibility, one that has the potential to make a difference in the lives of others and impact your own walk with Jesus as well. So, thank you for choosing to be a facilitator for your group.

Your role is to be the master of ceremonies by planning and guiding the meeting for the group's enlightenment and enjoyment. Everything you need is provided, so you do not need to teach or have all the answers. Your role is simply to facilitate the experience for the group.

In a study like this, you may have people who are interested in near-death experiences but are not sure about the God of the Bible. You may also have people who think NDEs are dangerous to even consider in the context of faith. The FAQs (page 123) can help you navigate some of these concerns, but remember that it's okay to create space for people to voice their concerns or questions. God often uses the process of people voicing doubts and struggles as a catalyst to help them grow a more rock-solid faith. So don't feel like you have to answer every question or concern. In fact, remind everyone to be respectful of diverse opinions and encourage them to continue reading the book, as many of their questions may find resolution along the way.

If you do have spiritual skeptics or those who do not yet follow Christ in the group, that's wonderful! Be vigilant to make sure they are not singled out or "preached at" by members of the group. Help them feel safe, loved, and encouraged by the group, and God will use the reading and discussion to draw them to himself. If needed, just redirect the conversation by saying something like, "Let's keep going and see what we discover," or "We have different perspectives, and let's respect that so that we can all learn together." Then move on.

Before the first meeting, make sure everyone in the group has a copy of the *Imagine the God of Heaven* book as well as this study guide. This will keep everyone on the same page and help the learning and discussions run smoothly and go deeper. The first assigned reading in the book and the personal studies follow the first group meeting, so let participants know that no preparation is required for Session 1. Everyone should feel free to write in their study guide and bring it to the group discussion each week.

SET UP

Here is a general guideline for how to budget your time depending on the length of your meeting.

Section	60 minutes	75 minutes	90 minutes
OPEN: pray and discuss the opening questions	10 minutes	10 minutes	15 minutes
READ: read the passage and reflect on key insights	10 minutes	10 minutes	10 minutes
WATCH: watch the video together and take notes	15 minutes	15 minutes	15 minutes
DISCUSS: discuss the questions based on the video teaching	20 minutes	30 minutes	40 minutes
CLOSE: reflect on key insights and pray together	5 minutes	10 minutes	10 minutes

Based on the needs and interests of your group, you may want to adjust the suggested times or eliminate some questions to allow for longer discussion of other questions.

As the facilitator, your primary responsibility is to create an environment that encourages learning and sharing. If possible, it's ideal to meet in a casual environment with comfortable seating, such as a family room or living room. Being in a home environment will help group members to feel more relaxed and open. Remember, a smile, a warm welcome, and simple refreshments will go far in creating an atmosphere conducive for group study and lively discussion. Note that you may want to consider arranging for childcare if your group includes parents of young children.

Wherever you choose to meet, you'll need to have a means of playing and watching the video together. This includes setting up a computer or DVD player and monitor. Set up and test all the equipment in advance to avoid potential disruptions to the meeting later.

OPEN

Open the meeting with a short prayer based on the focus for the week, and then use the discussion questions to get everyone engaged and thinking about the theme of the session.

READ

Ask a group member or two to read the Scripture passages for the session. After the reading, use the questions to engage group members in sharing their insights about the passages. It will be beneficial to hear from several participants in the group.

WATCH

Watch the video teaching. Encourage each member to take notes on anything that stands out to them and to write down any questions they might have.

DISCUSS

Encourage each member to participate in the discussion, but make sure they know it is not mandatory. (You don't want anyone to feel pressured.) As the discussion progresses, follow up with comments such as "Tell me more about that" or "Why did you answer that way?" This will allow for deeper reflections and invite meaningful conversations.

Note that you do not need to discuss all the provided questions. Feel free to pick and choose or to reorder the questions based on how the conversation goes. As the facilitator, be sure that no one dominates the discussion and that each person who wants to gets an opportunity to share. If you find someone is dominating, pushing an opinion, or stuck on a question, affirm their interest in that issue and then redirect the discussion. For example, "Thanks for sharing that. It's an interesting point/question. Let's move on, and we may find that this issue is addressed/resolved further into the study and reading."

CLOSE

Close by reading the encouragement paragraph and taking a few minutes for final reflections and prayer. Remind the group that the goal of the study is not just to read or talk about God but to engage with God in deeper ways. Thank everyone for coming and being a part of the group. Encourage them to read the assigned chapters from *Imagine the God of Heaven* and to complete the five personal studies for that session.

FAQs on NDEs

1. What is a near-death experience (NDE)?

A near-death experience can occur during clinical death, which is when the heart stops beating and all brain functions cease. When the person is resuscitated, they claim to have been conscious somewhere beyond their physical body, experiencing the life to come. These are referred to as "*near-death* experiences" because the person came back to life. Although such experiences have also been reported in cases without proof of clinical death, the stories in *Imagine the God of Heaven* focus almost exclusively on experiences for which there is evidence of clinical death.

2. Are there any biblical examples of near-death experiences?

I believe so. Consider this account of what happened to the apostle Paul: "They stoned Paul and dragged him outside the city, thinking he was dead. But after the disciples had gathered around him, he got up and went back into the city" (Acts 14:19-20, NIV). If a man is stoned to death and considered dead but gets back up and tells of an encounter with the God of heaven, that's an NDE. And this may be what Paul later described when he said of himself, "I know a man in Christ who fourteen years ago was caught up to the third heaven" (2 Corinthians 12:2, NIV).

Others who may have had an NDE include Lazarus (John 11:1-44), the twelve-year-old girl Jesus raised to life (Mark 5:35-43), the young man Paul raised to life (Acts 20:7-12), and the widow's son Elijah raised to life (1 Kings 17:17-24). We just don't have the stories of what they experienced while they were clinically dead. What we do know is that the Scriptures include testimonies of several people (such as Isaiah, Daniel, Ezekiel, Paul, and John) who had visions of heaven or were taken to heaven and saw God, and what they reported correlates with what NDErs commonly report today.

3. Why should we trust people who claim to have had a near-death experience?

While I do think NDE stories are evidence from God of his existence and the reality of heaven and hell, I do not advocate putting our trust in NDE stories. I want people to trust in God based on what he's revealed of himself in Scripture—and in *Imagine the God of Heaven*, I show how you can know that God inspired the prophets to write the Scriptures. I think it's better to see NDE stories as testimonies of God's existence and the reality of the afterlife, just as we would the testimony of someone who had a personal experience of God in their everyday life. We are wise to evaluate human testimonies based on how they align with God's self-revelation in Scripture. It's no different than what happened among people who saw Jesus heal people and raise the dead. Some concluded he was the Messiah, but others said his power to perform miracles came from Satan (John 8:48). NDErs interpret their experiences in light of their background and biases, as any of us would. That's why I'm not asking you to trust NDErs but rather to see how what they commonly report (as opposed to how they interpret it) aligns with God's revelation in Scripture.

4. The Bible says, "People are destined to die once, and after that to face judgment" (Hebrews 9:27, NIV). How should this inform our understanding of near-death experiences?

It's important to understand that a near-death experience is not full biological death or entrance into eternal life. A commonality of NDE stories is encountering a border or boundary that NDErs say they knew they could not cross and still come back to earth. In some cases, Jesus tells the person, "You have not died yet; you must go back." An NDE is not the same as crossing over into eternity—it's an experience somewhere between life on earth and the life to come. So when the Bible says, "People are destined to die once, and after that to face judgment," this refers to permanent death and eternal life. What NDErs experience does not contradict Hebrews 9:27 because they do not cross the boundary into eternal life but come back to earth. Further, the judgments spoken of in the Bible—the great white throne judgment (Revelation 20:11-15) and the so-called *bema* seat judgment pertaining to rewards for deeds done on earth (2 Corinthians 5:10)—don't happen until the conclusion of human history. So when NDErs experience a sort of life review in their NDE, this is not the same thing as God's judgment. Rather, it seems to be more a validation of Jesus' words that everything that is secret will be made known, even our secret thoughts and motives (Luke 8:17; 1 Corinthians 4:5).

5. **What about the Scripture passages that say no one has seen God? Shouldn't we reject these claims of NDErs who say they've seen God?**

Probably the most seemingly problematic statement relative to NDEs is Jesus' assertion that "no one has seen the Father except the one who is from God; only he has seen the Father" (John 6:46, NIV). A key principle of interpretation is to always interpret Scripture in light of Scripture. So, what must Jesus mean by saying, "No one has seen the Father," when Isaiah, Ezekiel, and Daniel all claimed to have seen God on his throne (Isaiah 6; Ezekiel 1; Daniel 7; Revelation 4)? Clearly, what NDErs claim to see does not contradict Scripture if what the prophets say aligns with Jesus' words. As I discuss in *Imagine the God of Heaven*, I believe Jesus is referring to the transcendent greatness of the infinite, eternal God whose being exceeds even what people in heaven can see or comprehend. Even in heaven we are not infinite in nature, so we can't "see" all of God. In that sense, no one has fully seen God except Jesus, the Son, who is one with God.

6. **Jesus said, "No one has ever gone into heaven except the one who came from heaven—the Son of Man" (John 3:13, NIV). Doesn't this discredit those who claim to see heaven in their NDE?**

On first take, this can be a confusing statement. Jesus would have been well acquainted with the Scriptures written by prophets such as Isaiah, Daniel, and Ezekiel who had seen heaven (which aligns with what NDErs see). In context, he's talking to Nicodemus, who also knew and studied the Prophets but was struggling to believe the mysteries of heaven Jesus was revealing. Likely, what Jesus is saying here is that either he is the only one who can come and go from heaven of his own accord, or he is making the point that he understands the ways of the heavenly Father in a uniquely intimate way because he is the one who descended from heaven. Regardless, NDEr reports align with something experienced later by John when God says to him, "Come up here," followed by John's report, "At once I was in the Spirit, and there before me was a throne in heaven with someone sitting on it" (Revelation 4:1-2, NIV).

7. **Is it possible that people who have had near-death experiences are being deceived by demons?**

Evil is real, and it's deceptive—on earth and in the afterlife. I found it interesting that many Christian NDErs I interviewed told me they had a welcoming committee of people whom they knew were there to guide and *protect* them on their journey to heaven. I always ask, "Protect you from what?" They don't know, but they intuitively knew in their NDE that those who came to meet them were there to protect them from something. So it appears that NDErs need protection, possibly from demonic interference, and without that protection could possibly be deceived by the demonic. How do we discern whether an NDEr has been deceived? By checking what they say with Scripture. God has given much evidence that the prophets and Jesus spoke his words of truth. I've given ways we can know God spoke through the prophets in *Imagine the God of Heaven*. So, we should always evaluate what NDErs say against what Jesus and the prophets taught. In some cases, I believe it's also possible that NDErs can have a "truthful" experience, but later interpret that experience in ways that evil twists into partial truths, leading them and others away from following God.

8. Can NDE stories be useful in pointing people toward God?

I believe that NDE stories are a gift from God to our globally connected world. They are testimonies from around the world of God's identity, love, forgiveness, and compassion that align with what the Bible teaches. I believe these stories provide a line of evidence for a new apologetic, capable of pointing people everywhere to the God who created us all for his love. These stories are well known and widely studied. What's missing is helping people see how they align with God's revelation, which is what I try to do in *Imagine the God of Heaven*.

9. Aren't you in danger of adding to Scripture by giving credence to these extra-biblical reports, some of which seem pretty wild?

Not at all. I like to think of NDEs not as new revelations but as enhancing the picture the Bible has already given us with more vivid color and detail. In other words, they enhance the understanding of the information we already have. An analogy would be watching a beautiful sunset from the shores of Hawaii while meditating on the verse, "The whole earth is full of his glory" (Isaiah 6:3, NIV). The beauty of the surroundings isn't providing new revelation but providing vivid clarity and color that enhance the biblical truth that the world is full of God's glory. If an NDEr says something that does not align with Scripture, reject it.

10. **How can you endorse the validity of NDE reports when some have gone on to occult practices or contacting the dead? Doesn't this prove all NDEs are deceptions meant to lead people away from the Bible and Jesus?**

It is true that some who have an NDE come back and seek out occult-like practices. But others come back, seek God, and find faith in Jesus. This should not surprise us since those who watched Jesus do miracles during his earthly ministry also had differing responses—some believed in him, and some denounced him. Every good gift from God can be twisted by evil. For example, while sex is a good gift from God (read Song of Songs), people have caused much harm by misusing it. Does that mean sex is evil? No, it means we should help people see what God intended when he gave us the gift of sex. The same is true with NDEs. They are meant to be a gift to help us discover that God is who he says he is and that he loves us.

11. **How do you account for those who see God or Jesus in their NDE but are clearly not believers prior to dying?**

It is not unbiblical for nonbelievers to see the risen Jesus. The apostle John wrote, "Every eye will see him, even those who pierced him" (Revelation 1:7, NIV). Paul was an unbeliever when he saw this same God of Light, who then identified himself as Jesus. And Paul was not converted just because he saw Jesus. In fact, Jesus did not share the gospel with Paul but only told Paul, "Go into the city, and you will be told what you must do" (Acts 9:6, NIV). Once there, it was a disciple named Ananias who told Paul what to do to be saved. Paul still had a choice. So it should not surprise us that unbelievers see the God of Light and Love and feel loved, yet God does not make the gospel clear in their NDE. God has always used people to tell other people about him, and he wants us to first make the choice to seek him; then we find him.

12. Don't NDEs promote universalism, that we're all going to heaven regardless of belief?

Not at all. There are heavenly NDEs, and there are hellish NDEs. If anything, NDEs clarify the reality of all that Jesus taught. It's also important to realize that NDEs are not indications of someone's final destination. I may be invited to visit Buckingham Palace, but that does not mean I'm being adopted into the royal family to live there forever. NDEs are just visits, not permanent residence. So we can't draw conclusions about who goes to heaven or hell based on their NDE. I found in my research that some NDEs start off wonderful, and if they had ended there, the NDEr would have concluded, "Atheists go to heaven." But then the person realized they were being deceived and were led into an outer darkness similar to what Jesus warned about. That's why I'm trying to show how NDEs fit within the bigger picture of God's revelation.

13. Paul wrote, "Satan disguises himself as an angel of light" (2 Corinthians 11:14). How do we know the God of Light NDErs encounter is not a deceptive spirit?

I'm not sure if Paul was being literal or metaphorical here. The context in which he made the statement is discerning false teachers, so it could be Paul is referring to "light" in the sense that Satan can cloak his temptations to make them appear to be good. For example, when Satan tempted Eve, he appealed to her by saying that eating from the forbidden tree would make her wise like God, knowing good and evil. He pretends he's bringing us light, yet his temptations enslave us in darkness. But if Paul meant that Satan literally appears as an angel of light, I am certain Satan could not also disguise himself to the point of conveying God's attributes. Many NDErs say things like, "This God of Light is the pinnacle of all love in whose presence I've never felt such overwhelming love."

Love comes from God, and Satan rejected God's love and leadership and was cast out of heaven. Jesus says Satan is a murderer and a liar, and Jesus implies that evil is incapable of love (see John 8:42-44). So it's hard to imagine that the God of Light and Love NDErs encounter is Satan disguised as God. However, it's also true that someone can encounter the true God of Light and Love in an NDE yet still be deceived into a false understanding of what their NDE means. Again, that's why it's so important to first understand the bigger picture of God's revelation throughout history so we can wisely discern NDE stories.

Notes

1. A. W. Tozer, *The Knowledge of the Holy* (New York: Harper & Brothers, 1961), 9.
2. *NIV Exhaustive Concordance Dictionary*, s.v. *"kōl," "lēbāb,"* Bible Gateway Plus, accessed March 14, 2023, https://www.biblegateway.com.
3. "Most Christian Countries 2023," World Population Review, accessed April 14, 2023, https://worldpopulationreview.com/country-rankings/most-christian -countries.
4. "The Top 20 Countries Where Christianity Is Growing the Fastest," Movements, June 10, 2015, https://www.movements.net/blog/2015/06/10/the -top-20-countries-where-christianity-is-growing-the-fastest.html.
5. Joe Carter, "The US Sends—and Receives—More Christian Missionaries than Any Other Country," Gospel Coalition, February 20, 2012, https:// www.thegospelcoalition.org/article/the-u-s-sends-and-receives-more-christian -missionaries-than-any-other-count/.
6. C. S. Lewis, *Mere Christianity* (New York: Macmillan Publishing, Co., Inc., 1943, 1978), 108.
7. Philip Yancey, *Disappointment with God: Three Questions No One Asks Aloud* (Grand Rapids, MI: Zondervan, 1988), 60.
8. Tim Keller, *Romans 8–16 for You* (Charlotte, NC: The Good Book Company, 2015), 201.
9. Swidiq changed his name to Cedric when he became an Anglican priest. His book, *I Once Was Dead*, is thus by Cedric Kanana, but his given name is Swidiq.
10. Cedric Kanana with Benjamin Fischer, *I Once Was Dead: How God Rescued Me from Islam, Drugs, Witchcraft, and Even Death* (Chicago: Oasis International, 2022), loc. 111–112, Kindle. Used with permission of Oasis International and Cedric Kanana.
11. Kanana with Fischer, *I Once Was Dead*, loc. 115–116, Kindle.

12. *The Lion King*, directed by Jon Favreau (Walt Disney Pictures, 2019), Yarn, https://getyarn.io/yarn-clip/acefbf92-61fa-4eb6-b736-7ad0e283ad2a.
13. Santosh (Sandy) Acharjee, *My Encounter with Jesus at Heaven's Gates: A Life-Changing Near-Death Experience* (Bloomington, IN: AuthorHouse, 2016), loc. 210–218, Kindle. Used with permission.
14. Dr. Mary Neal, personal interview with John Burke, Austin, Texas, February 22, 2016. Used with permission.
15. Fr. Cedric Pisegna, *Death: The Final Surrender* (Houston, TX: Passionist Publications, 2013, 2022), loc. 78–79, Kindle. Used with permission.
16. *"Phroureō," Thayer's Greek Lexicon*, accessed on Blue Letter Bible, https://www.blueletterbible.org/lexicon/g5432/kjv/tr/0-1/.
17. Penny Wittbrodt, Zoom interview with John Burke, September 28, 2022. Used with permission.
18. Everett F. Harrison, "Romans," *Expositor's Bible Commentary, Abridged Edition, New Testament*, Kenneth L. Barker and John R. Kohlenberger III, eds. (Grand Rapids, MI: Zondervan, 1994), 544.
19. C. S. Lewis, *Letters to Malcolm: Chiefly on Prayer* (New York: Harcourt, Brace and World, 1963; New York: HarperCollins, 2017), ch. 17.
20. Rebecca Ruter Springer, *Intra Muros* (Elgin, IL: David C. Cook Publishing, 1898), 91.
21. *NIV Exhaustive Concordance Dictionary*, s.v. "mā`ôz," accessed March 27, 2023, on Bible Gateway Plus, https://www.biblegateway.com.
22. "Derry KRK," Near-Death Experience Research Foundation (NDERF), undated, https://www-nderf-org.translate.goog/Finnish/derry_krk.htm?_x_tr_sl=fi&_x_tr_tl=en&_x_tr_hl=en&_x_tr_pto=sc. Translated from Finnish. NDERF excerpt used with permission of Jeffrey Long and Jody Long, founders and administrators of the Near-Death Experience Research Foundation.

About the Author

John Burke is the author of the *New York Times* bestseller *Imagine Heaven*, along with *Imagine the God of Heaven*, *No Perfect People Allowed*, *Soul Revolution*, and *Unshockable Love*. He and his wife, Kathy, founded Gateway Church, a multisite church based in Austin, Texas, that helps people explore faith. As an international speaker, John has addressed hundreds of thousands of people in thirty countries on topics of leadership, spiritual growth, and the exhilarating life to come. John and Kathy have two children and two grandchildren.

JOIN JOHN BURKE AND DISCOVER THE GOD WHO LOVES YOU DEEPLY AND IS CLOSER THAN YOU COULD EVER IMAGINE.

What nearly seventy near-death experiences reveal about the God of heaven

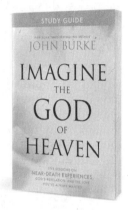

Great for small group or individual study

DVD to accompany the study guide with teaching from John Burke

A concise guide to commonly asked questions about near-death experiences

TO CONNECT WITH

JOHN **BURKE**

SEARCH ONLINE FOR
"AUTHOR JOHN BURKE"

SPEAKING EVENTS

BOOKS

CONTACT

OTHER FREE RESOURCES